PRAYERS
for the
CHURCH
COMMUNITY

PRAYERS
for the
CHURCH
COMMUNITY

Compiled by
Roy Chapman
and
Donald Hilton

Published by:
National Christian Education Council
Robert Denholm House
Nutfield
Redhill RH1 4HW

ISBN 0 7197 0205 4

Typeset by Surrey Graphics Ltd, Dorking, Surrey
Printed and bound by Page Bros (Norwich) Ltd

CONTENTS

Part 1   THE CHRISTIAN YEAR

        Advent   1 — 11

        Christmas and Epiphany   12 — 32

        Lent   33 — 75

        Holy Week and Easter   76 — 104

        Pentecost   105 — 114

        Trinity   115 — 118

Part 2   THE CHURCH

        The church community   119 — 169

        Life and mission   170 — 184

        Special occasions   185 — 213

Part 3   GENERAL PRAYERS

        Discovering God's world   214 — 227

        Christian life-style   228 — 249

        Christian discipleship   250 — 259

        People around us   260 — 289

        Education   290 — 297

        Community life   298 — 302

FOREWORD

This collection of prayers is offered to those who lead the worship of the Church, and especially to those ministers and lay preachers for whom this is a regular and weekly responsibility.

The compilers believe that it is helpful to see the local church as a single community of people binding all ages together in living friendship. Therefore the majority of the prayers can be used when all age-groups are present together, although a few are better suited to adults alone. The range of subjects included reflects the compilers' aim to offer prayers which speak to the essential needs and opportunities of each church community.

The compilers are jointly responsible for the authorship of nearly a third of the prayers and they are grateful to the many others who have allowed their work to be included. No uniformity of style has been imposed on the contributors and it is hoped that the resultant variety will make the collection useful in a large number of local situations.

In each section of the collection, and for ease of use, the prayers are presented in the following liturgical order: Invocation, Adoration, Penitence, Thanksgiving, Supplication, Intercession and Dedication. All the Biblical quotations included in the prayers are from the New English Bible.

As a former General Secretary of the National Christian Education Council, Roy Chapman has visited many churches of different denominations. Donald Hilton is the Moderator of the Yorkshire Province of the United Reformed Church. They have both used these prayers in their own ministries and hope that this has given the collection a sense of realism which will enrich the worship of the Christian Community.

Part 1
The Christian Year

ADVENT

1   You came, Lord Jesus, to save people from being afraid, to
release them from ignorance and foolishness, and to show
them how to love. Come again into our lives to save us from
all that makes life dull or frightening, and help us to live for
others, as you did.

2   Already, our Father, we are beginning to think about
Christmas. Gifts and cards, decorations and nativity plays,
preparation at home and church and school: we look forward
to them all and know they will bring their own special
happiness. As we are reminded about the birth of Jesus, help
us to understand what we are doing and to see the important
reasons behind all our activities and preparation. May we be
ready for Christmas when it comes so that we remember the
birth of Jesus with great thanksgiving, hearing again the
message of your love.

3   God our Father, we are part of your great family. In Jesus
Christ you came to the world as one of us, and through him
we know of your love and care. Be with us now and accept
the praise we bring. Help us, in our prayers, to think about
others as well as ourselves; teach us, through the reading of
the Bible, and through our thinking and our doing, the way
you want us to live; build us up into a happy and caring

family of your people that others may see in us that love that came into the world through Jesus.

4   Lord Jesus, we come to worship you. On this special Sunday we begin our preparations to celebrate your coming to our world. Be with us now, and help us to know your nearness not only in the time spent here in church but at every time of our life. Over the long years people prepared for your coming; they looked for a king and a conqueror, and when you came as a baby they missed seeing you; when you came with the conquering power of love they rejected you. Let us not miss your coming now, here in our worship and out in the world.

5   We remember at this time, Lord Jesus, how you came to disturb the world, and to turn the lives of men to God. You brought love to those who were unloved; hope to those who had nothing to look forward to; peace to those who were full of anxious daily cares.

But you also brought judgement to those who thought they were good men; to those who were content with their own lives; to those who looked down on other people and were sure that they knew everything about God.

Come into our lives, Lord Jesus, to turn us again to God, to help us to see ourselves as we really are and to take away from us all that is unworthy, so that we may share in your kingdom and know the joy of your presence.

6   We are late again: unprepared for Christmas and unready to meet its annual demands. The shops are overcrowded; the bargains gone, and time is running out. Presents are not wrapped, some unbought; the house is undecorated, and the Christmas tree naked. We are late again, unprepared and unready.

But, Lord, more serious yet: we are unprepared for the Christmas of your coming. We have neglected the anticipation of prayer; failed to see the signs of the times; disdained the fellowship of other Christians in regular worship, and turned aside from the Advent footpath of hope. We have sung carols as an ancient ritual, heard the stories without understanding, and used this season as no more than a peg on which to hang our passing pleasures.

Come, Lord Jesus, come!
Come into our complacency and stir us to action.
Come into our insensitivity and sharpen us.
Come into our false busyness and give us a word of peace.
Come into our lack of preparation and show us the true foundation of this season.
Come into our Christmas and make it your nativity.

7   Father God, we are sorry for those things in our lives which have hurt other people, ourselves and you.

In Jesus Christ we have seen the way in which we should love others, and we have not loved them. Jesus showed us how much he cared for needy people, and we have not cared enough. Jesus said that he had not come to be served but to serve, and we have not followed his example.

Forgive us when we have let you down, and as we now prepare to celebrate the first coming of Jesus, may we know that he is always with us, giving us the encouragement we need to follow him more faithfully every day of our lives.

8   Father God, at this time of Advent we prepare to celebrate the coming of Jesus into the world. As we think about his first coming we know that we are unprepared for his coming in the events of today and every day. He comes to us in those who are needy and unloved, in the people we find it hard to love. Forgive the things we have done and said which have

hurt others and hurt you. Forgive the things we have not done which have left people still in need, uncared for and unloved.

Father God, at this time of Advent we give thanks for the written word of the Bible, the record of the long years of preparation for the coming of Jesus: the gospels that help us to see Jesus; the story of the beginnings of the Church. Too often we ignore the Bible, we forget to read it, we do not trouble to find its meaning for us today. Forgive our neglect and our failure to find what you are saying to us through the Bible.

Father God, at this time of Advent we remember good men and women who, down the years, have spoken out the message of Jesus. Too often we have been silent and missed the opportunities to share the message of love which Jesus gave to the world. Forgive us those silences.

Father God, in the name of Jesus, who came to show us a new way to live, forgive us and help us by your presence to be your people both in word and deed.

9   Candles burn brightly in Advent to remind us of the joy that came into the world through Jesus Christ. But when Christmas is over the candles will burn low and die out.

We rejoice at all the colour and light of Advent and Christmas, but rejoice the more because the true light of Christ can never be extinguished.

Come into our lives, Lord Jesus, and light a flame of love that will never die.

10   Eternal God, we give thanks for this familiar time of Advent which, leading us to Christmas, brings well-loved stories and ideas to us again.

Give us the aid of your Spirit that we may look at the familiar and receive its message afresh. Do not let what is so well known to us obscure the new truth waiting to break into our minds, but take us deeper and deeper into the meaning of the incarnation of our Lord Jesus Christ that we may find new joy, new confidence and new hope.

In the name of Jesus, the babe who became our Lord.

11   Lord Jesus, you were given the name Immanuel, which means 'God is with us'. Be with us as we live our lives, that we may truly know that God is with us.

Lord Jesus, you came as a teacher to show the way we should live. Teach us how to love you, and how to love our neighbour as ourselves.

Lord Jesus, you came as a healer and you gave new life to those who were ill in body, mind and spirit. Help us to care as you cared, and to see you in everyone in need, that as we minister to them we may know that we continue your work of healing.

Lord Jesus, you came as a friend and called men and women to be your friends. We believe that you call us. Help us to answer you, to follow and to love you with all our heart.

Lord Jesus, you came to give yourself for the world, so that the world might know and love God. Help us to give ourselves to you. Be with us as our Master and our Lord, our teacher, healer and friend, for ever.

CHRISTMAS AND EPIPHANY

12   Lord Jesus Christ, you came to a stable when men looked in a palace; you were born in poverty when we might have anticipated riches; King of all the earth you were content to visit one nation; Creator of the universe you accepted the hills and plains of Galilee as the backcloth to your ministry. From beginning to end, your life held men in suspense, and its surprise forced them to reconsider their values and priorities.

Come to us, Lord Jesus. Do not let us take you for granted or pretend that we ever fully understand you. Continue to surprise us so that, kept alert, we are always ready to receive you as Lord and to do your will.

13   Love came down at Christmas, and that love was seen in Jesus. May that love be with us now.

Peace came down at Christmas, and that peace was seen in Jesus. May that peace be with us now.

Joy came down at Christmas, and that joy was seen in Jesus. May that joy be with us now.

May love, peace and joy be in our hearts as we celebrate the coming of God to his people, in Jesus Christ our Lord.

14   God, our Father, you have given Jesus Christ to be the Light of the world, so that all people may know the way to live. We welcome his coming and ask that, like wise men of old, we may offer our worship, and be glad in your presence.

15   Father, fill our hearts with joy and happiness as we come to celebrate the festival of the birth of Jesus. As our thoughts turn towards Bethlehem give us your spirit of love, that we may worship as shepherds did of old. Let us be open to your coming among us, so that Jesus may be born in our hearts. Be with us now and with all who worship you at this season, for the sake of Jesus.

16 Following each bidding, the response is: *We praise your name, O Lord.*

Let us praise God for the events of the first Christmas.

For his humble birth: the swaddling clothes and the manger in the stable:
We praise your name, O Lord.
For the message of the angels: good news and great joy to all people:
We praise your name, O Lord.
For the shepherds who came with haste, who saw the baby and glorified:
We praise your name, O Lord.
For the wise men who rejoiced when they found Jesus and brought gifts of gold, frankincense and myrrh:
We praise your name, O Lord.
For the quiet serenity of Mary who kept all these things and pondered them in her heart:
We praise your name, O Lord.

Grant, O Lord, that as we read the familiar stories again we may respond with love and gratitude and ever praise your name.

17 The light of the star drew them on:
wise men travelling with gifts,
for a fellow wise man and a king.

The Light draws us on:
Jesus, Light of the world, draws us
to give our precious treasures,
and to give ourselves.

And the Light gives us light:
it shows us the way,
it shines before us to encourage us,
it shines through us for others,
leading them to find its source themselves.

This is light; true light; the Light of the world;
 the light that is a way of peace, hope, justice and
  forgiveness;
 love in a darkened world;
 and the way to God, Father of us all.

18 Let us be glad, and with shepherds bring our adoration, for
God has given us his gift of Jesus.

Come to the manger, see the child Jesus, God's own son.
Welcome this heavenly guest, given as a baby so that we can
see and know how much God loves his world.

Let our carols of praise ring out in thanks to God, for it is
Christmas and, in Jesus, God is with us.

19 God has given to us his son Jesus; God is with us now and for
ever; God has come to us and calls us to be his people, his
family on earth. For this gift we celebrate at Christmas, we
bring our thanks and praise to God. God, we love you
because you have loved us, and you have shown your love in
Jesus Christ, whose birthday we now share.

20 Father, we thank you for all the things we *see* at Christmas:
 for candles and lights on the tree;
 for bright shop windows, for plays and pictures.

Father, we thank you for all the things we *hear* at Christmas:
 for our favourite carols and for church bells;
 for friendship's 'Happy Christmas', for laughter at parties.

Father, we thank you for all the things we *taste and smell* at
Christmas:

for Christmas dinner, pudding and cake;
for chocolates and sweets, fruit and nuts.

Father, we thank you for all the things we *touch* at Christmas:
for secret presents in hiding-places;
for mysterious parcels in the Christmas stocking.

Father, we thank you for all the things we *learn* at Christmas:
for reminders to appreciate our families and friends;
for the Bible stories about the birth of Jesus;
for the appeals to care for others;
and for the message of your great love for all people.

Thank you, God, for Christmas.

21   Let us praise God for all we receive at Christmas.
For gifts of many kinds that bring us pleasure;
for surprises planned to delight us;
for people whose kindness and thoughtfulness make us
glad:
we thank you, heavenly Father.

For children, with presents kept secret till Christmas
morning;
for parents, giving generously to make their children
happy;
for all exchanging and giving of gifts:
we thank you, heavenly Father.

For your many gifts that bring joy and gladness to our
lives;
for your greatest gift, Jesus Christ your Son, our Lord;
for the example, sacrifice and generosity of his life:
we thank you heavenly Father.

Teach us, O God, that it is a joy both to give and to receive.
In our giving make us thoughtful and generous; in our
receiving make us glad and grateful.

22   Glory to God in highest heaven, and on earth his peace for men on whom his favour rests.

We thank you, God, for the greatest gift you have given to us in the birth of Jesus your Son.
We thank you that he came humbly and without fuss, and that shepherds came to see him and worship him. We thank you that we can worship him and share together the happiness of this festival.

We thank you for Mary and Joseph and their care of him. We thank you that, when Jesus grew up, he shared with us your love, and that in his life we find our way to live. We thank you that he is always with us, born in us today, and ask that we may show our thanks by loving you and loving those around us, not only at Christmas but every day.

23   Lord Jesus, wise men from distant lands visited you as a child. We thank you that people from every part of the world can share your love and be your friends.

You received gifts of gold and frankincense and myrrh. We thank you that you are always glad to receive the gifts your people bring: the gifts of love and service, the gifts of caring and compassion, the gift of work well done.

Receive us today with our gift of thanksgiving for the happiness that Christmas brings; our thanksgiving for the promise of today that you are among us, sharing in our festival; our thanksgiving that Christmas, your coming to the world, is not for one day only but for every day of the year.

24   Thanksgiving and praise to God!
Eternal God, the gates of heaven were raised in Bethlehem.
Jesus left the place of glory to live with men.
We rejoice that he came,
    not in military power to subdue us,
    nor yet in glory such as would blind our eyes,

nor yet in such majesty as would set him apart from us,
but left the gates of heaven as a child in helplessness,
 to be born as we were born,
 suckled by a human mother, watched over by a human
  father.
 and so recognised by us.

Thanksgiving and praise to God!
Eternal God, the gates of heaven are raised eternally; the
doors are open for ever.
In Christ you have made an open road for us,
 valleys between heaven and earth are levelled,
 impassable mountains are brought low,
 none now need stumble along the heavenward path as
  Christ pioneers the way to eternity for us.

Thanksgiving and praise to God!
Eternal God, you strengthen us in our pilgrimage,
 you give us daily bread of body and spirit,
 you grant us to be one with the fellowship of believers,
 you journey with us in close companionship.
Raise the gates of our hearts, O God,
break down the stubborn doors of our spirits,
and come and reign among us.

25   At this time we remember the story of the wise men taking
gifts to the baby.

Father God, if Jesus were a baby now we would give him
gifts. Help us to know that giving gifts to others, especially
those whose need is great, is like giving a gift to Jesus and
that it makes you glad. Help us to know that we can give ourselves to Jesus by learning about him and letting him teach
us how to live.

26   Let us remember how the coming of Jesus meant different
things to different people. To Joseph it brought great
perplexity, and to Mary both glory and pain; the shepherds

were surprised by joy, and the wise men confirmed in hope; Simeon found contentment in it, and Herod a threat. By their response, they revealed the real and secret thoughts of their inmost hearts.

O God, grant us the humility to hear the word Christ wants to speak to each one of us in his coming, knowing that in his holy presence nothing in us can remain concealed. Hearing his word may we receive his cleansing, and our hearts become temples worthy of his dwelling.

27 Lord Jesus, be born in us today. Give to us your spirit of love, that shows itself in loving others. Let our giving at this time reflect the gift of your coming among us as a gift of God. May we know the gladness and the joy that inspired shepherds to visit you. May we have the vision and insight that inspired wise men to bring you their gifts, and may we not only love the Child of Bethlehem but follow faithfully the Man of Nazareth, Jesus Christ our Lord.

28 Lord God, wise men were guided by a star to Jesus: so let your love be our guide, always leading us in our daily life. As the wise men gave gifts of gold, frankincense and myrrh, help us to offer our prayers and our worship, our obedience and our love, our skills and our talents, for your praise. And as wise men found the Christ as a child, born as one of us, so too may we find him in our work, in our play, in our homes and in every part of life. So by your coming may every part of life be hallowed and made special.

29 Father, we've been looking forward to Christmas for weeks, and now it's come at last! It is a lovely day, and we're going to enjoy every minute of it! But please help us not to be so busy enjoying it that we forget all about other people.

As we spend today in the comfort of our home, may we
    remember people who have no home;
as we laugh and play and talk and eat with our family and
    friends, may we remember people who are alone, with no
    one to care about them;
as we enjoy our food and drink, may we remember people
    who are hungry and starving;
as we open our presents, may we remember people who are
    very poor;
as we enjoy today, may we remember people who are too ill to
    enjoy it;
and as we remember, make us more determined to do
something to help them.

30   O Lord Jesus Christ,
you were homeless in the moment of your birth:
    look with mercy on the hungry and homeless of our world
    today.

You were a refugee fleeing from political persecutors:
    look with mercy on all those displaced by war or hounded
    by governments and forces who seek to deny them their
    freedom.

You were rejected even before you were born and often
dismissed throughout your life:
    look with mercy on those who feel rejected by society and
    lack friends to give them hospitality and love.

You still suffer with your people:
    look with mercy on us all.

31   Lord Jesus Christ, we celebrate your birth among us. You
lived in our real world, and knew its hardship and its need.
You showed love for lonely people, outcast people, people
who were ill or unloved. So we bring you our prayers for
people in need today, believing that you love them now as
you did then.

We pray for homeless people; for refugees who have no country to call their own.
You were born in a stable because there was no room for you in the houses of Bethlehem, and you were taken to Egypt as a refugee when Herod threatened your life.
Let your blessing be with those who work to help homeless people and refugees, and give to all of us the determination to help where we can, so that every family on earth will have a place of which they can say, 'This is my home'.

We pray for lonely people: those who are lonely because they have lost their partner; those who are lonely because no one seems to care; those who are lonely because of handicap or illness.
You offered friendship to people like Zacchaeus and a Samaritan woman; you know what it is like to be lonely, and you welcomed the friendship of the disciples, and Mary and Martha.
Let your presence be with those who are alone at this season of friendship, and may we take your friendship to those whom we know will be alone at Christmas.

We pray for children everywhere.
You grew up in a family with brothers and sisters, and one day you called children to you and gave them your blessing.
Bless our children today. In the enjoyment of this holiday may they experience something of those deep joys you want for all your children, young and old.

We pray for the world.
You came as the Prince of peace and brought a message of peace for all people.
Help us to be peacemakers, in our homes, at our work, wherever we meet with people, so that your Spirit can work through us in our community and in the world.

We pray for your church.
You have called us to be part of your family. Be with us now and always; give us strength to do your work well, and may the spirit of Christmas show itself in us, as we serve and love and care for others in your name.

32   Heavenly Father, as we celebrate the birth of your Son, we bring to you in his name the needs of the church and of the world.

We pray for the church:
>for the Christian family celebrating this festival in so many different ways, and for those who dare not celebrate openly;
>for Christians in countries where there is persecution;
>for Christians in our own country, with whom we share our celebrations;
>for our church family.

Help each of us to be glad of your presence, and to rejoice at the coming of Jesus. Give to us the help we need to be loyal and faithful, knowing that with your power nothing need make us afraid.

We pray for peace in the world:
>for countries where there is war;
>for places where there is hatred between races;
>for the leaders of the nations.

By your Spirit among us may bitterness and hatred be cast out, and the peace and goodwill of Christmas find a place in the hearts of all people.

We pray for people in need:
>for those who are ill;
>for the lonely and bereaved;
>for the refugee and the homeless;
>for the hungry and the poor.

Be near to all who especially need your love; let your Spirit be with those who care for them, and give to all of us the desire to help when and where we can.

We pray for our families and friends:
>for those away from us today;
>for those who have asked our prayers;
>for those who will join us in our family parties.

In all our celebrations, in our eating and drinking, in our giving and receiving gifts, in all we do at this time, may we remember him whose birth we celebrate, and give thanks for his coming.

LENT

33   Lord and Master, how patient you were:
      with people who were slow to understand you;
      with the disciples when they squabbled about unimportant
          things;
      with those who wanted to follow you, but dared not risk it;
      with the men who plotted against you;
      with Peter who denied you, and Judas who betrayed you.
Lord and Master, how patient you were, caring more about others' good than your own. Help us to learn your way.

34   Lord Jesus Christ, we rejoice that you were born into this world as we were born, and then lived a life knowing human joy and sorrow, human hopes and fears and, at the end, a human death. Your life is very close to ours and we know you as a real and living person. No story-book character could help us as you help us. No bright idea in a man's mind could support us as you support us. No law, however excellent, passed by a government could change us as you change us. You are one of us and so we understand you as you understand us. You deserve our praise and we gladly offer our adoration.

35   Lord, you refused no one who came to you for help or forgiveness. When people crowded around seeking for healing, you did not spare yourself. When they came early, stayed late, and left little time for meals, you did not send them away. When they broke in on your privacy, you showed no impatience. When they brought their children, you received them gladly. Yet, Lord, we are often too busy to see the needs of those about us. If we loved as you love, we would see and care and find time.

Fill us with compassion, Lord, like your compassion, and help us to dedicate to you our time and our skills.

36   Lord Jesus, we recognise you as a friend who faced hunger, thirst and human problems, as we do. When we read of your life and see the chance meetings, the accidents, interruptions and the humour, we see our own lives reflected.

Forgive us that so often we allow these things to interrupt and disturb us rather than using them as opportunities to proclaim your love. Give us the quality of life that takes every incident and happening and sees its potential for good.

37   What are we giving up for Lent?
Sweets... smoking... some luxury or another?

Forgive us, O Lord, when we cheapen self-denial, thinking that the rejection of accustomed luxuries is all you require of us. Help us, rather, in costly service and self-forgetfulness to lay aside the sins which so easily beset us and to run a better race for you.

38   Following each bidding the response is: *We thank you, Father God.*

For calling Jesus from his home and work as a carpenter:
We thank you, Father God.

For equipping him to help all kinds of people and to speak to them:
We thank you, Father God.

For his security in your love which set him free to serve:
We thank you, Father God.

For the faith his call gave to the first disciples:
We thank you, Father God.

For the influence of Jesus in our lives inviting us to share the joy of your kingdom:
We thank you, Father God.

39   Following each affirmation the response is: *We thank you, Lord.*

Let us thank God.

For the heavens that declare your glory, and for the earth you have made so fair:
    We thank you, Lord.

For the glory of the sunshine and the clear air, and for health to enjoy them:
    We thank you, Lord.

For the shapes of the hills and trees, for the colours of the flowers and of the seas, and for sight to enjoy them:
    We thank you, Lord.

For the songs of the birds, for the music of voice, and for hearing to enjoy them:
    We thank you, Lord.

For the books of all ages, for poetry and music and art, and for a mind to enjoy them:
    We thank you, Lord.

For those who have conquered evil, for their faith and hope and courage, and for the power to follow them:
    We thank you, Lord.

For those who have loved us and cared for us, and asked only our love in return, and for a heart to love them:
    We thank you, Lord.

For Jesus Christ, our mighty deliverer and King, for a heart to love him and a life to give to him:
    We thank you, Lord.

40   Teach us, O Lord, how to say 'no' to ourselves. It is so natural to want our own way. When wanting our own way ignores other people's needs and is not your way for us, make us strong enough to put self aside and do your will.

41   Lord Jesus Christ, you know the needs of human life. We ask
you to help us as we seek to live our lives according to your
example.

Help us by your presence to overcome our hasty speech that
hurts others; to be free from greed and selfishness, from
pride and jealousy, that spoil our life.

Help us by your presence to curb our temper, to be free from
moodiness and wanting only our own way.

Let your presence help us to care about the feelings of others,
to be gentle, and ready to say we are sorry.

Lord, you saw deep into the hearts of those who were around
you. You knew the arrogance of Peter, the pride of James
and John, the hatred of your enemies. But you never stopped
loving, and sought to bring the best out of them.

You know us, Lord. Bring the best out of us, so that our lives
may reflect your way for the world.

42   Lord, when you walked on earth, you told men to look
around them to find God. And men saw the beauty of earth
and sky, of flower and field.

When we look around we often see factories, and chimneys,
and houses, and cars, and we forget that the world belongs to
God.

Help us to see signs of God's presence in our modern world:
in the wonders of science,
in the discoveries we have made,
in finding and using the resources of the earth.

Above all, let us be the people in whom God is seen,
giving him thanks for every good gift,
sharing his bounty with others.

So may the whole world join in praise, and all people have
the full life you came to give.

Boyhood of Jesus

43   It is the baby we remember; the baby who was just like any
other baby and yet was God indeed.

It is the boy we remember, growing up like every other boy,
knowing the joy and pain of growth and slowly learning more
of himself and of God.

It is the young man we remember; sometimes angry,
sometimes uncertain, sometimes knowing, sometimes
searching, but always holding the presence of God in his life
and standing alongside ordinary people in love and
compassion.

It is Jesus we remember; may the memory refresh us and
bring us closer to you, O God, with thankful adoration and
grateful praise.

44   Lord Jesus Christ, because of the kind of man you grew up to
be, we believe that you must have been brought up in a
happy and united family. We want our families to be like
this. Forgive us when we spoil family relationships. We
criticise too much and say 'Thank you' too little. Sometimes
we are jealous and rude, lazy and thoughtless. We often want
too many possessions and too much attention. We are truly
sorry. Make us more ready to learn from you the secret of a
loving heart and an unselfish life.

45   Lord God, we are glad to know that your Son, Jesus, lived as
a boy, sharing experiences common to us all.
       He laughed and cried,
       worked and played,
       listened and talked,
       learned and loved,
              just as we do.
We are glad to remember that whatever our experiences in
life, Jesus understands them, for these were his experiences,
too.

46 Jesus, you lived as a boy in your home in Nazareth; bless our
homes and protect our families.
Jesus, you lived under the authority of earthly parents; build
bridges of tolerance and understanding between the
generations in our homes and families.
Jesus, you lived in a carpenter's household; may we help each
other to do our daily work honestly and wholeheartedly.
Jesus, you were content to be brought up quietly and without
the limelight; make us ready to be unselfish and
undemanding in our homes, that our service to others may
be service to you.

Jesus the worker

47 We remember Jesus the carpenter.

He learned a trade under the watchful eye of Joseph.
He followed his trade as breadwinner for the family.
His work was good, never skimped, never careless.
He remembered those who would use his work, both people
and animals.
He knew the satisfaction of making something well.

Help us, Lord Jesus, to follow your way in the work we do.
Encourage those whose jobs are monotonous and dull with
the knowledge that they, too, are serving their fellow men.

48 Carpenter of Nazareth, whom God called from daily work to
serve him as preacher and teacher, healer and comforter,
hear our prayer for all your people as they work in your
name.

We pray:
for those called from their accustomed pattern of work to
prepare for a lifetime of service in the Christian
ministry;

for those who, as lay pastors and lay preachers, hold in one
concern their place in society and their ministry to the
people of God;

for those who bring their leisure time as an offering to God
as they care for children, lead youth activities, prepare a
ministry of song, serve on committees, visit the elderly,
or perfect our stewardship of buildings and money.

Lord Jesus, skilled alike in shaping wood and fashioning the
lives of men and women, receive the work we do in each part
of our life and make us workmen who do not need to be
ashamed, so that all we do may become a living sacrifice to
your name.

49   Lord Christ, you worked as a carpenter at Nazareth: let your
blessing be upon our daily work.

We pray that, in our various callings, we may do our work as
an offering for you to accept. Take our skills, our talents, our
duties and our service, and use them for the good of all
people.

We pray for those who serve us by their work: for those by
whose work we are fed and clothed, housed and warmed; for
those who make our life comfortable and pleasurable; for
those who serve us in shops; and those who use their skill and
strength to bring us goods from other lands.

May all our work be part of your creative work for mankind,
and may we so order the life of our country and of the world
that all people are able to make their contribution to the
welfare and good of others.

The temptations

50   Eternal Father, we have known you from the beginning, for
all that may be known of you lies plain before our eyes. Your

everlasting power and deity have been visible to the eye of reason ever since the world began. And yet we have refused to honour you as God and to render you thanks.
Father, forgive us.

Lord Jesus Christ, the testimony to your life has always been before us. Men heard you, saw you with their own eyes, looked upon you and touched you with their own hands. And what they saw and heard they declared to us to make our joy complete. Yet we still doubt and have failed fully to see the meaning of your earthly life.
Lord Jesus, forgive us.

Holy Spirit of God, you have encircled us from the moment of our birth. We experienced the harvest of your presence in the love of parents, the joy and peace of our homes, the patience and fidelity of friends and in our own spontaneous urge to gentleness and self-control. And yet still we live as though the material things of life define our total being.
Spirit of God, forgive us.

Grant that we who so readily fall to temptation, ignoring our Father, neglecting the Son, and blinding ourselves to the presence of the Spirit, may yet grow into that truth which will enable us to know even as we are known.

(Based on Romans 1.20-21; 1 John 1.1-4; Galatians 5.22)

51   Lord God, we are sorry for the ways in which we have hurt you. We have trusted in the things of the world, and believed that they could give us everything we needed for a full and wholesome life. We have looked for the praise of other people whenever we have tried to help those in need, and we have neglected to do good things that no one else would see or know about. We have loved money and possessions so much that they have become like a god to us.

Father, forgive us, and help us to stand firm when we are tempted to live in these ways. By the Spirit of Jesus, your

Son, make us more truly your children; finding our true life in you; serving and loving and caring, not for praise or thanks but simply because that is your way; using our money and possessions wisely and unselfishly, and in all things giving you thanks.

52   Lord Jesus Christ, we recall that at the start of your ministry you were tempted to use your power in the wrong way, and to induce people to follow you for the wrong reasons. Thank you for refusing to give in.

We remember, too, how your friends later tried to persuade you to take the popular way and how, in Gethsemane, you were tempted to turn back from the cross. We rejoice that your love was strong enough, your courage great enough, to resist. And now we see you as the one who understands us in our temptations. Thank you, Lord.

53   Lord Jesus, you were tried and tempted by the forces of evil. They tried to make you use:
    popularity instead of faithfulness;
    fame instead of service;
    power instead of sacrifice.

These temptations still come to us, Lord. We are far weaker than you. Lord Jesus, give us strength to shun them, as you did. May we choose the way of:
    faithfulness rather than popularity;
    service rather than fame;
    sacrifice rather than power.
Then we shall be of use to God and man, as you were.

54   O Jesus Christ, you have called us to be disciples in your school; help us to learn from your experience and follow your example.

Teach us how to recognise the approach of evil in all its varied forms and to be on our guard against it.

Because you were tempted in your life, may we never be ashamed of temptation in our own, but save us from the weakness that gives way to it.

In time of need make us strong, and reassure us that your support is close at hand.

Help us so to walk and talk with you each day that we may grow ever more like you, our Lord and Master.

55 Lord Jesus Christ, when you had the power to command others you chose to use your power in service. When you could have silenced all opposition you allowed even your enemies to have their say. When you could have forced your will you chose to persuade with love. We call you 'our Lord' but you give lordship a new meaning. We say 'Christ the King' but we have never heard of another king like you. In birth and life, in death and rising, you have given us a new interpretation of human experience and evoked new hope in us.

Help us, so that what we see in your life may be increasingly introduced into our own.

56 Look in mercy, and offer your help O God,
   to those who carry burdens so great that they are tempted to lose heart;
   to those who feel themselves driven into a corner with no room left for manoeuvre, and are tempted to give up;
   to those whose life seems to be in the hands of others offering no opportunity for their own decisions, and are tempted to surrender;
   to those struggling to maintain a crumbling relationship, and are tempted to accept defeat as inevitable;

to those who face death with no more hope than they faced
life, and are tempted to reject God and themselves.
For all these, and especially for those who have lost the will
to pray for themselves, we offer these our prayers.

The disciples

57   Sometimes, Lord, you must have been disappointed in the
twelve men you chose to be your disciples:
    they became angry when children were brought to you;
    James and John had tempers;
    Peter was rash and conceited;
    Thomas doubted;
    Judas betrayed you;
    and, at the end, most of them fled when you hung on a
      cross.

But you never gave them up. You stood by them during your
life and you came back to them from the dead to give them
your Spirit. Your compassion is tireless; your patience is
never defeated; and your love lasts for ever.

58   Lord Jesus, we remember the men you chose as your disciples:
    Simon Peter, the outspoken man who denied you;
    Andrew, James and John, whom you used to win others;
    Matthew, the unpopular tax-collector;
    Thomas, who doubted you;
    Simon, the revolutionary Zealot;
    Judas Iscariot, who betrayed you;
    Philip, who wanted to see God;
    Bartholomew, James and Judas, quietly working in the
      background.

Jesus, thank you for taking ordinary men and using their
gifts in your service. It gives us confidence that we too may be
useful to you.

59   After each sentence the response is: *Lord, speak to us.*

Lord Jesus, you called Simon and Andrew as they mended
their nets;
Lord, speak to us.

You called James and John as they worked alongside their
father;
Lord, speak to us.

You called Matthew as he sat at his daily work;
Lord, speak to us.

You called Paul as he travelled along the road;
Lord, speak to us.

You have called countless men and women into your service
through past centuries;
Lord, speak to us.

Lord, grant that we are not so busy in this noisy world that
we fail to hear you when you call us. When we hear you,
whether we are at work or play, with friends and families or
alone, may we respond to your call with enthusiasm,
obedience and love.

60   After each affirmation, the response is: *Lord, may we do
your will.*

Jesus said, 'Not everyone who calls me "Lord, Lord" will
enter the kingdom of Heaven, but only those who do the will
of my heavenly Father.'
Lord, may we do your will.

Jesus said, 'Love your enemies; do good to those who hate
you; bless those who curse you; pray for those who treat you
spitefully. Treat others as you would like them to treat you.'
Lord, may we do your will.

Jesus said, 'When you do some act of charity, do not
announce it with a flourish of trumpets. Your good deed

must be secret, and your Father who sees what is done in
secret will reward you.'
Lord, may we do your will.

Jesus said, 'If you dwell in me, and my words dwell in you,
ask what you will, and you shall have it. This is my Father's
glory, that you may bear fruit in plenty and so be my
disciples. As the Father has loved me, so I have loved you.
Dwell in my love. If you heed my commands, you will dwell
in my love, as I have heeded my Father's commands and
dwell in his love.'
Lord, may we do your will.

Jesus said, 'This is my commandment: love one another, as I
have loved you. You are my friends, if you do what I
command you. This is my commandment to you: love one
another.'
Lord, may we do your will.

Jesus said, 'Full authority in heaven and on earth has been
committed to me. Go forth therefore and make all nations
my disciples; baptise men everywhere in the name of the
Father and the Son and the Holy Spirit, and teach them to
observe all that I have commanded you. And be assured, I
am with you always, to the end of time.'
Lord, may we do your will.

Grant us, Lord Jesus, that we may always think and do those
things that are according to your will for us; that we may be
your faithful disciples, all the days of our life.

Jesus the friend

61 No shadow darkens the friendship you offer to us, Lord Jesus
Christ. No trivial mood or passing fancy alters the constancy
of your compassion. No wind of change blows, first hot then
cold, to blight the love you offer. You call us your friends and
your deed is as good as your word.

Thanksgiving, praise and adoration is our glad response to
you, our friend and Lord.

62   We have friends. Thank you for them, Lord.
But some of them forget us, and you never do;
and some of them are unkind to us, and you never are;
some of them are real friends one day, and act like
        enemies the next, but you are always the same.
Thank you, Lord Jesus, for your unfailing friendship. Help
us to be as loyal to you as you are to us.

63   Lord Jesus, you do not call us servants; you call us friends
and that is good news indeed!

When people are depressed may they hear the good news of
your compassion.

When people are anxious may they learn of your care.

When people are afraid may they know that nothing can
separate them from your love.

May your love disperse anger and hatred and renew love and
faith so that, being your friends, we may be friends with each
other.

Jesus the teacher

64   Our Father God, forgive us that, like the prodigal son, we
accept all that you give us, then use it for our own ends.

Forgive us that, like the elder brother, we will not accept
other people, but want to keep them at arm's length; that we
judge them and think we are good compared with them.

Forgive us that we think the worst of people, so that we fail to
accept them as you do.

May the picture of you that Jesus drew for us become more
vivid in our lives, so that we may reflect your goodness, your
love and your care for all.

65   To the prayer: *Thank you for your teaching,* the response is:
Help us to practise it.

Happy are those who know they are spiritually poor: the
kingdom of heaven belongs to them.
Happy are those who mourn: God will comfort them.
     Thank you for your teaching. *Help us to practise it.*

Happy are the meek: they will receive what God has
promised.
Happy are those whose greatest desire is to do what God
requires: God will satisfy them fully.
     Thank you for your teaching. *Help us to practise it.*

Happy are those who show mercy to others: God will show
mercy to them.
Happy are the pure in heart: they will see God.
     Thank you for your teaching. *Help us to practise it.*

Happy are those who work for peace among men: God will
call them his sons.
Happy are those who suffer persecution because they do
what God requires: the kingdom of heaven belongs to them.
     Thank you for your teaching. *Help us to practise it.*

Lord, may we forget ourselves and find true happiness
through serving you and serving others.

(Based on Matthew 5.3-10)

66   We thank you, O God, for the teaching ministry of Jesus, for
his patience with those who were slow to learn, and his
simplicity which all could understand.

We need that patience, for we ourselves have been slow to
learn. Give us the teachable spirit so that, as we read his
words, we may understand and, having understood, may
have the will to obey.

67   Following each affirmation the response is: *Lord Jesus, we praise you for all you are to us.*

Jesus came, proclaiming the Gospel of God and saying, 'The kingdom of God is upon you; repent, and believe the Gospel.' Let us praise him for the promises he makes to us.

Jesus said, 'I am the light of the world. No follower of mine shall wander in the dark; he shall have the light of life.'
Lord Jesus, we praise you for all you are to us.

Jesus said, 'I am the bread of life. Whoever comes to me shall never be hungry, and whoever believes in me shall never be thirsty.'
Lord Jesus, we praise you for all you are to us.

Jesus said, 'I am the good shepherd; the good shepherd lays down his life for the sheep.'
Lord Jesus, we praise you for all you are to us.

Jesus said, 'I have come that men may have life, and may have it in all its fullness.'
Lord Jesus, we praise you for all you are to us.

Jesus said, 'I was dead and now I am alive for evermore. Be assured, I am with you always, to the end of time.'
Lord Jesus, we praise you for all you are to us.

May the grace of the Lord Jesus Christ be with us all.

68   Lord Jesus, the news that you bring about God is very precious; there is no other news which can compare with it.

Help us to value all you tell us like a pearl of great price, and be ready to put it before every other concern in our lives.

Help us to see what we must give up, so that we can live in the light of all you want us to know.

69   Lord Jesus, we feel our faith is small and our achievements for you even smaller. But you taught us that size does not matter; even something as tiny as a mustard seed grows into a large bush. May this prove true of our faith and service, so that the good work you have begun in us may one day be perfected.

70   Lord Jesus Christ, the world is in great need of your message and love. There is misunderstanding between young and old, argument between nations, a great divide between the rich and the poor, a hurtful gap between the hungry and the well-fed, and mistrust between workers and management in industry. We need someone to show us how divisions can be healed, gaps closed and reconciliation achieved.

We hear your teaching and we see your life. The stories of your birth show us workmen-shepherds and wise men worshipping together; your group of disciples shows us men of differing ability and belief united in service; your death evoked a response which cut across the usual division of Jew and Gentile; and the gift of your Spirit created a new community able to step across ancient barriers with gaiety and ease.

Lord Jesus Christ, we need someone to come to help us in our world today. From your teaching and your life we believe you are the one to do it.
Come, Lord Jesus.

71   Jesus taught us to pray, 'Forgive us the wrong we have done as we have forgiven those who have wronged us.'
Let us think in quietness what it is we ask in such a prayer.

Jesus said, 'If you forgive others the wrongs they have done, your heavenly Father will also forgive you; but if you do not forgive others, then the wrongs you have done will not be forgiven by your Father.'
Silence

Jesus said, 'If your brother wrongs you, reprove him; and if he repents, forgive him. Even if he wrongs you seven times in a day and comes back to you seven times saying, "I am sorry", you are to forgive him.'
Silence

Peter asked Jesus, 'Lord, how often am I to forgive my brother if he goes on wronging me? As many as seven times?' Jesus replied, 'I do not say seven times; I say seventy times seven.'
Silence

Jesus said, 'When you stand praying, if you have a grievance against anyone, forgive him, so that your Father in heaven may forgive you the wrongs you have done.'
Silence

Jesus said that he who is forgiven much, loves much, but 'where little has been forgiven, little love is shown.'
Silence

If we claim to be sinless, we are self-deceived and strangers to the truth. If we confess our sins, he is just, and may be trusted to forgive our sins and cleanse us from every kind of wrong.

Jesus the healer

72   We marvel, Father of love, at the stories we read of the ministry of Jesus. Blind men were given their sight, lepers were restored to health, the lame walked, and those obsessed by fears found calm and peace.
We give thanks to the Lord, the healer.

Our wonder and thankfulness is no less when in our present day you work through the skill of the surgeon's hands, the perceptive insight of the doctor, and the care of nurses.
We give thanks to the Lord, the healer.

Marvellous too, O God, is the power of your Spirit that overcomes the selfishness in mankind enabling us to care for

those in need through a welfare state, drawing on the
resources of the healthy to meet the needs of the sick.
We give thanks to the Lord, the healer.

73   Lord, your touch brought healing and encouragement
to many people. Give us grace to be your servants in our time.
May our hands be gentle to those in trouble, strong to those
in weakness, and ever willing to be offered in friendship.

74   Lord Jesus Christ, you healed many who were blind and lame
and suffering from all kinds of illness. We believe your
healing power is as great as ever, and we ask for such
concern for others as will enable them to receive comfort and
hope and recovery of health. Take our thoughts and prayers,
and use them to further your work of healing today.

75   Jesus of the healing hands, lay them now on any distressed in
body, mind or spirit. Shock us out of our lack of caring so
that our hands may become your hands, strong to heal. May
we never add to the sufferer's burden by offering pity. May
we never hinder your healing purpose by dwelling on their
weakness, but instead take into every situation your calm
and peace and assurance.

HOLY WEEK AND EASTER

Palm Sunday

76   Lord Jesus Christ, we respect your low profile entry into
Jerusalem; in such a way you came to Bethlehem, and in

such a way have you entered our own hearts. Quietly, discreetly and without fuss, you came anonymously but with great persuasion.

In such a way help us to witness to you in our world today. The limelight advertises you less effectively than the gentle candle of faith; shouting your name from the rooftops antagonises the man in the street; the foot-in-the-door gospel salesman finds his goods suspected; the big battalions deafen the quiet enquiry; and the strident evangelist leaves no time for questions.

But still you enter your Jerusalem today.
> Quiet faith,
> persistent service,
> the life of integrity,
> compassion to the deprived,
> justice for the disadvantaged,
> bread and wine;

all these lay their palms in homage and love before the king who wears no crown.

Lord Jesus, we respect the low profile of your entry into our lives.
Come in your quietness and reign for ever.

77   Lord Jesus, we remember how you came to Jerusalem ready to face death.

We praise you for your courage,

> because you came to the city of danger
> > without a great army to fight for you,
> > without any magical powers to get you out of trouble,
> > only with a patient, forgiving love;
> because you did not make men listen
> > by physical force,
> > by words spoken in anger,
> > by making them afraid;
> because you would not use any other way but love,
> > even if it meant dying on a cross.

Come to us today with the same love, and set us free to follow
you on the Jerusalem road.

78   A donkey king!
Were there those who laughed?
Did some scorn?
How many turned their head, embarrassed?
What of the anger of those who saw a sacred prophecy
abused?

But now, O Lord, with the hindsight of the cross, it makes
sense to us, so we are glad:
glad of the applause of the crowd who trusted their first
reactions and welcomed their donkey king,
glad of the shouts of little children caught up in a sense of
celebration,
glad that there were those who glimpsed, fleetingly, the
nature of a king who straddled a donkey.

Donkey King, we join the throng, we raise a voice of child-
like praise and trust, we glimpse the secret of your reign.
Welcome to our Jerusalem!

79   Lord Christ, we sometimes think that your enemies were very
wicked people; and then it comes as a shock to us to realise
that what we think are the small sins in our lives were big
enough to cause your death.

You faced the anger of men who were afraid because their
unworthy ways of living were being exposed.

You faced the jealousy of men who felt that their leadership
in religion and law was being undermined.

You faced the hatred of men who believed that political
security was better than a clear conscience.

You faced the pride of a nation which did not want to hear it
was being disloyal to its appointed task.

Anger, jealousy, hatred and pride are things we know a
for they are part of us. By your refusal to allow these sins t
have the last word against your love, come into our lives and
deliver us.

80   Lord,
like us, you did not know the future.
You came to Jerusalem
ready for pain and death,
but not knowing how or when.
Be with us
when we don't know what is in store for us.
Help us to face the things that make us afraid.

81   We remember at this season, O Father, the sufferings of our
Lord. We thank you for all that we have gained because he
faced the cross. May we so follow him that the suffering we
have to bear may bring blessing to others.

82   Lord Jesus, you showed them!
In one clean sweep of righteous anger
   you shattered their self-confidence,
   overturned their tables,
   upset their cash registers,
   and sent the doves and pigeons fluttering!
Profiteering, bribery, greed, prejudice — in your Father's
house. Over the years your anger had built up, until it found
the right moment to express itself. It had to.
Lord Jesus, you showed them!

Lord, we feel like that sometimes.
We see it all happening:
   the poor down-trodden,
   the aged forgotten,

ly ill misunderstood and avoided,
y unheard and unfed,
n the street becoming a statistic or a number.
l happening.

hen and how to act.
Give us e courage of our convictions.
Do not let us relax in the cause of justice and truth.

Good Friday and Passiontide

83 Jesus! Carrying your own cross!
Was it worse than being made to dig your own grave?
You were nailed to the cross and they made you carry it first!

You must think a lot of us to have done that.
Help us to think a lot of you.

84 Lord Jesus Christ, you told your disciples that the greatest
expression of love is that a man will give his life for his
friends. You have called us your friends, and you have given
your life for us. When we think about this we are filled with
wonder and amazement that you would do this for us! In
return, we can only offer our love and ask that this time of
worship will express what we feel in our hearts, and be
accepted as our gift to you.

85 O Jesus Christ, we remember that as you hung upon the
cross you prayed for the people who put you there. Lord, we
find it hard to forgive those who hurt us. We want to hit
back, and so often we do. Help us to see the forgiving spirit
as a sign of strength and not weakness. Let your example be
our inspiration, and your Spirit our constant companion.

86 Lord Jesus, the disciples ran away from you when you needed them most; Peter denied you when challenged that he was one of your friends; Pilate washed his hands of you; the soldiers mocked you; the crowd rejected you, and you were crucified.

These are the events we remember today. In many different ways we too have run away from you, denied you, washed our hands of you, mocked and rejected you, and we are sorry. Forgive us.

Come to us now, as you came to your first friends, to Peter and the other disciples, and give us the chance to begin again. Let your Spirit be with us, so that when we are tempted to fail you again we shall be strong enough to stand firm.

87 To the words: *For the victory of your love,* the response is: *We offer our thanks and praise.*

Lord Jesus, we know how cruelly you were treated:
you were falsely accused, convicted, beaten and mocked.
  Yet, for the victory of your love:
    We offer our thanks and praise.

Nailed to a cross, you were defenceless and alone;
friends had deserted you, enemies despised you.
  Yet, for the victory of your love:
    We offer our thanks and praise.

From all sides you received insults and hatred;
it almost seemed that God had abandoned you.
  Yet, for the victory of your love:
    We offer our thanks and praise.

You showed no hatred or scorn in return;
instead your words were, 'Father, forgive them.'
  Lord, for the victory of your love:
    We offer our thanks and praise.

88   Lord Jesus Christ, there is much that we are not able to
understand about your sufferings and death, but we can see
that what you did and what you suffered was because you
love us so much.
Thank you, Lord Jesus Christ,
for all the benefits you have won for us,
for all the pains and insults you have borne for us.
O most merciful Redeemer, Friend and Brother,
may we know you more clearly,
love you more dearly,
and follow you more nearly;
for ever and ever.

(Based on a prayer of Richard of Chichester)

89   Saviour Christ, it is a mystery to us that you had to die upon
a cross. We should like to believe that if you came today this
would not happen. But in our hearts we recognise that our
selfishness, apathy and pride would crucify you again.

You could have escaped your cross, but then we should never
have known the depth of the love you have for us. Therefore,
we thank you, Lord, that you accepted it, and loved to the end.
We dare to ask for grace that we may follow in your steps.

90   Lord Jesus Christ, you are 'the way, the truth and the life',
and by your triumphant death on the cross you gave these
words their full meaning.
Your way is not to leave us to struggle on by ourselves but to
    share with us all the love and resources of God.
Your truth is not limited to the sum of human knowledge,
    but is the truth of God's purpose for all things.
Your life is not confined by birth or death, but is everlasting
    beyond even time and space, and this present life you
    share with us.

Guide us in your way to find the strength of your company in all we do.

Encourage us by the truth of God's purpose to stand up amid all the tensions and distractions of modern life.

Fill us with the assurance of life everlasting that we may see our life not within the shallow limits of material things but against the backcloth of God's eternal love and purpose.

91   Lord Jesus, help us to walk with you along the way of the cross:

the way of humility,
the way of obedience,
the way of love.

Give us faith and courage to follow you all the way.

92   Father, we remember gratefully and humbly that Jesus bore the cross for us. Help us willingly to accept the cost of doing what is right, speaking what is true, resisting what is false, helping those in need, forgiving those who have done wrong and, in ways that each new day may demand, loving you and our fellows with all our heart and soul and mind and strength, so fulfilling your commandment.

93   The response is: *Lord, help us to understand and accept this.*

The way of the cross is seldom the obvious way;
those who follow it are often misunderstood:
Lord, help us to understand and accept this.
They are seldom applauded:
Lord, help us to understand and accept this.
They are frequently ridiculed:
Lord, help us to understand and accept this.
They are often lonely:
Lord, help us to understand and accept this.

The way of the cross is never a short cut:
  it can only be travelled in faith:
    Lord, help us to understand and accept this.
  It passes through every area of life:
    Lord, help us to understand and accept this.
  It is the way the Master went:
    Lord, help us to understand and accept this.
  It is the way that arrives with God:
    Lord, help us to understand and accept this.

94 To the prayer: *Speak to us now,* the response is: *And help us to follow you.*

Remember now the words that Jesus spoke from the cross.
Lord Jesus, you spoke a word of forgiveness:
  'Father, forgive them.'
    Speak to us now: *and help us to follow you.*
You spoke a word of compassion:
  'Today you shall be with me in Paradise.'
    Speak to us now: *and help us to follow you.*
You spoke a word of comfort:
  'Mother, there is your son. There is your mother.'
    Speak to us now: *and help us to follow you.*
You spoke a word of doubt:
  'My God, my God, why hast thou forsaken me?'
    Speak to us now: *and help us to follow you.*
You spoke a word of human need:
  'I thirst.'
    Speak to us now: *and help us to follow you.*
You spoke a word of victory:
  'It is accomplished.'
    Speak to us now: *and help us to follow you.*
You spoke a word of trust:
  'Father, into thy hands I commit my spirit.'
    Speak to us now: *and help us to follow you.*

Give us your strength, O Lord, that, walking in the way of your cross, we may share in the victory of your love.

95   Lord Jesus, through the Gethsemane of your broken heart
and the Calvary of your broken body, help us to trust you
when we have to face suffering and pain.

Through any suffering of ours let there come fellow-feeling
and compassion for others and a deeper sense of caring than
possesses us when we are well. Strengthen our faith through
endurance by trusting you when we can hardly see the way
ahead for tears. Guide us to the realisation that in
mysterious ways we can sometimes share your sufferings,
and even through our pain have a part in your redeeming
plan.

96   And when they came to a place called Golgotha (which
means 'Place of a skull') they crucified him.

Jesus, we think about you on your cross. It was not bad men
who put you there but people like ourselves. It is when we are
selfish, jealous, seeking only our own ends and forgetting to
love, that we crucify you.

You loved all people and told your friends that they must
love one another: we ask that, through our prayers, we may
remember those who need our love and care.

    Jesus, you opened blind men's eyes and made the deaf
        hear: be near to those whose world is dark or silent.
    Jesus, you healed a lame man and made him walk again:
        be near to those who are handicapped.
    Jesus, you healed a woman who had been ill for many
        years: be near to those who are in pain, and to those for
        whose illness there is as yet no cure.
    Jesus, you welcomed people of many races, you talked with
        them and helped them: be near to those who suffer
        because of their race or their religion.
    Jesus, you brought hope and love to those whom others
        thought hopeless and loveless: be near and speak your
        word of peace to those who cannot be reached by any
        words of ours.
    Jesus, you touched a leper and healed him: be near to
        those who are rejected, unloved and unwanted.

Jesus, you comforted a sorrowing mother: be near to those who are sad.

Jesus, we think about you on your cross. You went on loving even those who crucified you. Let your love flow through us, so that we may care as you cared, and love as you loved, always.

Easter

97   Jesus Christ is alive in the midst of his people here today!

Lord, help us to be sensitive to your presence;
give us ears to hear your word;
give us hearts to feel your love;
give us minds to understand your truth;
give us wills to practise what you preach;
and all to your glory!

98   O God our Father, on Easter Day we join with the members of your family all across the world to offer praise and adoration for Jesus — Jesus alive, powerful and victorious. We rejoice that in Jesus all that separates and injures and destroys has been overcome by what unites and heals and creates.

Lord, we want to be counted amongst the friends and followers of Jesus who in every age have received new life from him, have stood up for him, and given themselves to him.

99   We rejoice today, Lord Jesus, in the great triumph which you won on a hill called Calvary. When you died on the cross, everyone thought you had been defeated. All the hopes and dreams of your followers seemed ended. But now we know that they were wrong! The empty grave announced your victory. Death had been conquered and sin broken, and you had risen! Show us what this can mean for us so that we share the full joy of your resurrection life.

100 O God, our Father, you have shown us the power and majesty of your love in the cross of Jesus. We could never have seen it so clearly anywhere else. We thank you that love triumphed at last, despite man's sin and hatred and failure, and burst upon an astonished world on the first Easter Day, giving a joy which can never fade. Your love reaches us and we respond with thankfulness and praise.

101 O Lord, who came to live among men, you promised to be with us always. You are present in times of happiness and times of sorrow. We recognise you in the goodness of people about us and in those who are in need. You guide us when we turn to you for help and you speak to us through our knowledge of right and wrong. As you never leave us, may we never turn aside from following you.

102 Lord, we glimpse eternal life
in our joy at the sight of a baby, newly born;
in the look of wonder on a child's face;
in the care of a nurse for a patient;
in the joy of parents welcoming home their children;
in the dedication of a doctor, a teacher, a neighbour.

We give thanks and praise that in these experiences, and in many others, we see values that live on into eternity. Help us to live by these values, now and always.

103 Lord Jesus, you turned the despair and dismay of the disciples into joy and peace when you broke through the evil of the cross and made your followers sure of your victory. In that knowledge they found courage when they might have been afraid, hope when everything seemed to go wrong, and an overwhelming happiness when they would otherwise have known only sadness.

There are often things which make us afraid, things which go wrong, things which make us sad and sometimes full of doubt. Come into our lives with your joy and peace, and help us to share the victory of your presence, not only for our sake but so that your life may be seen in us.

104   *Spring*

O ever living God, creator and sustainer of all things; the days grow longer at your bidding; the rain is warmer at your command; seeds burst into life by your indwelling; birds and beasts respond to your ceaseless activity; the whole world of nature echoes your praise.

Grant, O Father, that we may rejoice with your creation and praise your name. Help us to see in the return of life to the earth a parable of how at this season Jesus, your Son, overcame sin and death. Grant, O Father, that our lives may be filled with his life-giving Spirit.

PENTECOST

105   Come, Holy Spirit:
inspire us with divine energy,
appoint us to your service,
and bless us with your gifts.

Come, Holy Spirit:
give us new life,
strengthen us in our loving,
and help us to see your way in life.

Come, Holy Spirit:
    refresh our tired lives,
    release us from all that hinders our growth,
    and guide us to peace.

Come, Holy Spirit:
    introduce us to God the Father,
    tell us about God the Son,
    and our praise will never cease.

(Based on Veni Creator Spiritus)

106 Creator Spirit, source of the dynamic energy in the universe, offer your power to recreate the Church, taking the seed of our hope to make new life.

Spirit of power, present in the life of Jesus who reached the full height of manhood, offer your power to the Church enabling it to reach its maturity.

Renewing Spirit, you swept through the group of disillusioned disciples revitalising them in fellowship, mission and service. Offer your power to the Church recalling us to the priorities of our life and task.

107 Lord, when your Spirit is at work things begin to move. He changes situations; he transforms lives; he is the divine energy at work in the world. Without him we are weak, we get nowhere, we are in the dark.

Let the power of your Spirit flow through us that we may come alive in Christ, be given strength beyond our own, and be enabled to do whatever he calls us to do.

108 For the inner spirit of power that lifts us when we are down; for the inner spirit of delight that restores joy in sadness;

for the inner spirit of light that dispels darkness;
for the inner spirit of truth that pierces ignorance;
for the inner spirit of love that conquers prejudice;
    we give thanks to the Spirit of God, source of all that is
    good.

109   We do not understand, eternal God, the ways of your Spirit
in the lives of men and women. He comes along secret paths
to take us unawares. He touches us in joy and sorrow to
make us whole. He hides behind coincidence to lead us
forward, and uses our human accidents as occasions for
influence. We do not understand, but we welcome his
presence and rejoice in his power.

110   The response is: *Holy Spirit of God, teach us to love.*

Love is patient; love is kind and envies no one:
    Holy Spirit of God, teach us to love.
Love is never boastful, nor conceited, nor rude:
    Holy Spirit of God, teach us to love.
Love is never selfish, nor quick to take offence:
    Holy Spirit of God, teach us to love.
Love keeps no score of wrongs:
    Holy Spirit of God, teach us to love.
Love does not gloat over other men's sins, but delights in the
truth:
    Holy Spirit of God, teach us to love.
There is nothing love cannot face:
    Holy Spirit of God, teach us to love.
There is no limit to its faith, its hope, and its endurance:
    Holy Spirit of God, teach us to love.
Love will never come to an end:
    Holy Spirit of God, teach us to love.

(Based on 1 Corinthians 13.4-7)

111   We remember, Lord, that one of the signs that your Spirit is at work in our hearts is that we show kindness in all our dealings with other people. Yet so often we have spoken the unkind word, and have been thoughtless in what we have said to other people and about other people.

Grant us your Spirit, so that day by day kindness may colour all we do, that in our lives we may reflect the true spirit of Jesus, who was kind to all, who loved good and bad, rich and poor, friend and stranger, and so made them realise that God is love.

112   To the prayer: *Lord, hear our prayer,* the response is: *And fill us with your Spirit.*

Lord, we thank you for the coming of your Holy Spirit to the disciples, filling them with power and knowledge and love.

May we know that power within our own lives, taking away our fear and inadequacy.
    Lord hear our prayer: *And fill us with your Spirit.*
May your Holy Spirit turn our unbelief into faith and fill our lives with your love.
    Lord hear our prayer: *And fill us with your Spirit.*
Grant that we, like the first disciples, may fearlessly proclaim your Gospel, and be ever obedient to your call.
    Lord hear our prayer: *And fill us with your Spirit.*

113   O God, how foolish we are when we trust only in ourselves! Help us to put our trust in you and to live by the power of your Spirit, so that we may do what is right, be courageous in times of difficulty, and follow Jesus Christ faithfully as his true disciples.

114   Holy Spirit, you came to us as a gift from God. Continue to come to the world with all your spiritual gifts.

Grant the gift of wisdom:
>to politicians and administrators in the world's planning;
>to businessmen and industrialists in the use of the world's
>resources;
>to arbitrators and negotiators in all human relationships.

Grant the gift of healing:
>to all involved in our hospitals and clinics;
>to all who seek to mend broken lives and torn relation-
>ships;
>to all who show love and understanding where healing is
>no longer possible.

Grant the gift of prophecy:
>to those who have their finger on the pulse of our needs;
>to planners and policy-makers who seek right priorities;
>to church leaders and members with a vision for the
>future.

Grant the gift of love to all people: the love which is never
boastful, conceited or rude,
>never selfish nor quick to take offence,
>never keeps a black-list of wrongs,
>but which is all-enduring, all-caring and all-embracing.

May these your gifts enrich the world and encourage us in
the work of Christ.

TRINITY

115   Celebration! That's what this is, Lord, and that's why we are
here!
>Give us gaiety of spirit now:
>>as we celebrate your father-love that makes sure that we
>>have everything we need for our life on earth;
>>as we celebrate your marvellous gift of Jesus to be our
>>Saviour and our life-long friend;

as we celebrate the promise of a life that goes way beyond
death into your heaven;
as we celebrate the Holy Spirit living within us and helping
us to live as we ought to live.
Give us celebration, Lord!

116   You are worthy of all praise, eternal Father:
you created the universe in all its variety
and you made us in your own image.
You are worthy of all praise, Lord Jesus Christ:
you visited the earth to reveal the Father's love
and you restored our hope by your living and dying.
You are worthy of all praise, Holy Spirit of God:
you gathered together the people of God
and you called us into the life of the Church.

Eternal Father,
Lord Jesus Christ,
Holy Spirit of God,
you are worthy of all praise.

117   In our creation and growth,
in the providence of his care,
in the promise of eternal love,
the Father has given his gifts to us.
Thanks be to God.

In the guidance of his teaching,
in the example of his life,
in his own life freely given on Calvary,
the Son has given his gifts to us.
Thanks be to God.

In our birth into faith,
in his comfort and strength,
in his leading into all truth,
the Spirit has given us his gifts.
Thanks be to God.

· **118** O God, Creator of all good and beautiful things, we give
thanks.

O Jesus, Saviour of all men, we give thanks.

O Holy Spirit, giver of life more abundant, we give thanks.

O ever-living God, coming to us in so many ways, yet always
the same, always bringing life, always bringing beauty,
always bringing joy, we give thanks.

To God the Father, the Son and the Holy Spirit, we evermore
give thanks.

Part 2
The Church

THE CHURCH COMMUNITY

119   Sunday is celebration day:
    the first day of creation;
    the day of Jesus' triumph;
    the day of the gift of the Holy Spirit;
    the first day of the new week.

Lord, help us to celebrate this Sunday:
    to rejoice in the gifts of your creation;
    to find new life in Jesus and his gifts;
    to set our sights on your way for the week ahead;
    to enjoy being your church in fellowship and worship.

Thank you, God, for this celebration day!

120   What here we celebrate, O God, in the life of this church is
    yours not ours. Yours its strength and hope, yours its faith
    and high endeavour. All is yours and you are all in all.

Take the strength and weakness of this church,
    and let both speak of your glory.

Take the hopes and fears of this church,
    and let both bring its people nearer to you.

Take the excitement and the routine of this church,
    and let both be means by which your work is done.

Now in worship we offer you your own.
Christ be praised!

121   Eternal God, we who meet in one church building in one town of one country remember now the millions of people who today, in many towns, villages and cities, offer you worship. Our language is different but our worship is one; different in nationality and race our praise is united. Let all the world join its praise so that one great chorus of adoration and love is offered up to you, our God and Father.

122   O God, you are always the same. Our fathers worshipped you and called you Father because they trusted you. Every generation has offered you worship believing in your constant love.

We now come, conscious of a changing world but more conscious of your unchanging power; aware of the fickle nature of our own devotion but more aware of the permanence of your care over all your creatures; sensitive to the uncertainties of human life but more sensitive to the certainties of your truth.

God of our fathers, you are our God and always will be.

123   Thank you, God, for letting us be together here in church.

We thank you especially because when we come we know that we are always welcome and find our friends here with us.

We want to praise you in our worship, to sing about your love for us, and read of all that you have done.

But most of all we want to learn more about Jesus: all the things he said and did so that, as we live, we can grow to be more like him.

Father, we like our church. We are glad that boys and girls, men and women, mothers and fathers, grandparents and friends, young and old, can all be together to worship you, and we ask your Spirit to help us as we sing, pray, talk and listen so that when we go home we take the happiness of our worship with us.

The church community

124 Heavenly Father, we pray for our church and thank you that there is so much friendship here. Show us how to help each other so that the worship we now offer is the worship of a true family, through Jesus Christ, who is the Head of the Church.

125 Father, every day you give us is a new day, with new things to do, new ideas in our minds, new people to meet and new sights to see. A new day is like a present you give us to enjoy; full of hours and minutes and seconds to fulfil our lives; time to share with other people. Forgive us for the days we have taken and spoilt; for times we have used selfishly as though they belonged to us alone.
Father, help us to use this new day to learn more about Jesus, to practise kindness to other people, to worship you and say our prayers together; so that at night-time we can say that this has been a good day, and offer thanks for it.

126 Lord Jesus Christ, you came to us in a way that we can understand.
You came as a child in your mother's arms, helpless and dependent.
You came as a boy with searching questions, eager to discover the meaning of life.
You came as a man in strength to lead us to truth and point us to the real issues of human existence.
And now you come to us in risen power through word and world, through worship and work.
In your coming in humility, Lord Jesus, you expose our failures, our foolishness and our pride. But in your coming you also give us hope for, from birth to death, you show us love facing hatred without despair. And in your coming you bring us joy and the promise of peace, for you are a brother to all men and your gentleness is the strongest power we know. Come now, Lord Jesus Christ. This is the appointed time. Claim your rights over us all and make your home with us.

127 Eternal Father, you are the God of new beginnings. You
never end. You never grow old. You are always beginning.
Like the love that springs from your heart to meet our need
you are new every morning; and when evening comes you
have not tired nor grown weary.

> You saw a beginning in the creation of the world when the
> universe came to its birth.
> You saw a beginning in the life and resurrection of our Lord
> Jesus Christ when death was swallowed up in victory.
> You saw a beginning in the struggle of the disciples to receive
> the gift of the Church which is his Body.
> You saw each of us in our own beginning, formed in the
> womb by your love and created to be your own.

Here and now we make a new beginning in worship. We
believe that you are with us as we begin.
Thanks be to God.

128 God, our heavenly Father, when we try to talk to you, we
sometimes feel that we must speak in a special way, and use
words that we do not really understand.

Help us to remember how Jesus taught his friends to call you
Father, because that was the most loving word he could use.

Then help us to speak to you in words we would use when we
share with close friends our joys and sorrows.

We believe that you are glad both to hear our prayers, and to
listen to our need.

129 So many gifts we receive, O God, through the ministry of the
Church: quietness, friendship, thoughtfulness, challenge,
stimulation, information and insight; so many gifts.

At one time or another, O God, we have all received these
gifts. You have taken the voices of men and women as your
own voice. You have taken silence and let it speak.

Conscience and the call to duty can pierce complacency in this place and, as minds act together, truth dawns.

Here the confusion of the world can be examined quietly; human conflict is set against the backcloth of your peace and in the search for human significance we encounter the life of Jesus.

Help us today, O God, that our longing for you may find fulfilment.

130 The risen Lord has promised to be with us.
  Silence
Lord Jesus, you are alive for ever.
You are here with us now.
Help us to be aware of your presence.
  Silence
Lord Jesus, you are alive for ever.
You are within us now.
Help us to welcome you.
  Silence
Lord Jesus, you are alive for ever.
We are still; speak to us now.
Help us to listen to you.
  Silence

Lord Jesus, whether we feel you near or not, you have answered our prayers. You are within us. You are around us. You are always renewing us by daily friendship and guidance. We have your promise that as we share your life, so we share your resurrection.
Thanks be to God for our risen, reigning Lord.

131 In a world torn by noise, and splintered by division:
  let your peace be known in this holy place.
In days destroyed by pressure, and fractured by strain:
  let your peace be known in this holy hour.

In personalities threatened by the foes of the mind, and in spirits menaced by guilt:
> let your peace be known in this holy worship.

132   Eternal God, whenever we talk about you we end up dissatisfied and uncertain, for our words are poor vehicles of the truth your being proclaims and even of the thoughts of our own minds.

Our stumbling phrases cannot capture the bright vision of your presence. Our little words burst at the seams by the might of your true word. Our experience of your love cannot be held in check by our clumsy phrases. For you are God eternal, almighty and full of power. You enter human life endlessly. You break the barriers of our words. You spring out of the creeds that think they contain you. Before the beginning, you are; and at the end, you still will be.

Eternal God, where words fail us, confront us with your presence. Be in our experience even if we neglect you in our words. Be in our lives even when we cannot recognise your presence. So that life and power and presence may joyfully proclaim the love that language can never comprehend.

133   Following the words: *We come to you,* the response is: *Lord, be with us.*

Eternal God, it is easy to feel afraid. There are known fears that trouble us: ill health, the fear of death, of pain, of disturbance. There is the unknown fear: the fear that springs out, the fear that grips the heart and erodes life.
In our fear we come to you.
> *Lord, be with us.*

Eternal God, we often feel the weight of our own sin and folly. We see the right and we can't do it. We know the

wrong and it comes so easily to us. We speak and wish we
had been silent; we are silent and wish we had spoken.
Friendships are fragile and even love can be perverted.
In our sin and folly we come to you.
Lord, be with us.

Eternal God, we are sometimes lonely in this world. In a
crowd our individuality is obtrusive; alone, we feel friendless.
Even the best of friends can misunderstand us and a curtain
can come between us and our nearest loved ones.
In our loneliness we come to you.
Lord, be with us.

Eternal God, there are times when we feel that evil will gain
the upper hand in this world. Force seems mightier yet and
power is in the wrong hands. Peace is destroyed and enmity
and prejudice triumph.
In our fear of the power of evil we come to you.
Lord, be with us.

Eternal God, we here and now affirm our faith. Nothing in all
creation, in earth or heaven above, can come between your
people and your eternal love.

134 Jesus said, 'I thank thee, Father, Lord of heaven and earth,
for hiding these things from the learned and wise, and
revealing them to the simple.'
We thank you, Father, that we do not have to be intelligent
or clever to know you. We just have to be humble and aware
of our need. We have to be poor in spirit, completely
dependent on you, Father. Then we will be wise.

Paul said, 'God has made the wisdom of this world look
foolish... the world failed to find him by its wisdom, and he
chose to save those who have faith by the folly of the Gospel.'
We know how much you care for us because of the life and
death of Jesus, our Lord. We know our Lord is risen. We
know your forgiveness. We know your Holy Spirit is with us
to guide us and make you real to us. We know that Christ
lives in his Church and therefore in us. We know that if he is

with us we cannot die but have eternal life. There is nothing
more we need to know, Father. You will take us on from
here. Grant us this true wisdom and with it the peace and joy
which is Christ's promise to all who follow him.

135 O Lord, it is good to be alive in your world. It is good to wake
refreshed after a night's sleep. It is good to breathe in the
fresh air at the start of a new day. It is good to feel our bodies
fit, strong and healthy to face the tasks of the day. It is good
to see the sights and hear the sounds of your world. Help us
never to lose a sense of wonder for all that you have given us.

136 The earth spinning in space; the sun bright with burning; the
stars flickering across the heavens; how great is the universe
and vast its power!

Lord God, whose mind is greater than all we can ever see or
discover in telescopes and space probes, we praise you for
being with us in Jesus Christ, teaching us that in all the
greatness of your creation there is no one unnoticed,
unwanted or unloved.

137 O God our Father, forgive us our sin of self-indulgence.
We are ashamed to remember how we have been ruled by our
appetites, when we knew that, by your Spirit, we might and
should have ruled them.

We have slept when we should have wakened; we have rested
when we should have worked; we have eaten when we should
have fasted; we have enjoyed ourselves when we should have
given enjoyment; we have stayed at home when others
needed us; we have set our own interests above our brother's.

We cannot now reclaim the opportunities of service we so
guiltily lost. Our brother has suffered, and we ourselves have

suffered too. We know it, and are ashamed. By your forgiveness waken a new and a right spirit within us, making us tireless and cheerful in self-sacrifice.

138 Heavenly Father, you have a plan for your world and we each have a part to play in it. Forgive us that we hinder your purpose, not only by doing wrong, but also by not doing the good we should. Forgive us that we relapse into a self-centred concern for our own ease, rather than put ourselves out to help others. Forgive us that our love of ease keeps us from the strenuous service you ask of us. Forgive us that our lazy minds choose easy platitudes rather than thinking through eternal issues. Grant us such a zest for following Christ that we may be ready to strive to our utmost for his sake.

139 Father, too often we ask for great gifts from you but know in our heart of hearts that we would not use them even if you showered them upon us.

We ask for strength to serve others;
   but we barely use the strength you now give us, or spend it on ourselves.

We ask for deepening love;
   but the love we now show is too readily tainted by selfishness.

We ask for adventuring faith, boldness of thought;
   but keep our feet firmly fixed in trackbound paths.

We ask for courage;
   but decline to face up to opportunities which would allow us to show it.

We ask you to be present in all our days;
   but we know we would hide if you truly came amongst us.

We ask to be made whole;
> but enjoy too much the ease and comfort in which our
> fragmented human nature allows us to rest.

And yet these are the gifts we seek: strength and love, faith
and courage, an awareness of your presence and the
wholeness of our humanity. The prayers we offer are more
true than the lives we live. The gifts we seek are more truly us
than the weakness we show. Lord, hear our prayers.

140 To the versicle: *Forgive us, O Lord,* the response is: *And
help us not to fail again.*

We have not always told the truth about ourselves:
> making ourselves out to be better than we are;
> pretending to remember something when we have forgotten
> it;
> claiming we can do more than we can really cope with:
> Forgive us, O Lord. *And help us not to fail again.*

We have not always told the truth about other people:
> pretending that they are not as good or clever as they really
> are, because we envy them;
> telling tales about them without realising how much they
> may be hurt:
> Forgive us, O Lord. *And help us not to fail again.*

We have not always told the truth about you, O Lord:
> because we have been afraid of being laughed at;
> because we have accepted what others have told us without
> thinking for ourselves;
> because we have not taken enough trouble to learn about
> you:
> Forgive us, O Lord. *And help us not to fail again.*

141 Father, we thank you for the church and its people, and
gladly acknowledge all the gifts you have given us through its
life.

Here in the church we saw the dawn of our faith,
here we were led in the search for deeper faith,
here we offered the early strains of our worship and the surer
    notes of growing praise,
here we were strengthened in our desire and ability to serve,
here we have seen need and been given the opportunity to
    respond;
and so our thanksgiving for the church is strong and true.

But we are sad,
    sad that the church has lost so many of its opportunities,
    sad that early enthusiasms have been dimmed,
    sad that our faith has not always been strong enough to
        meet necessary change,
    sad that our courage has sometimes failed before the unex-
        pected.

And so, with thanksgiving and with sadness, we bring the
church to you; the church we know here and the greater
Church of all nations and races.

    Grant light, that we may see the way to which you are
        calling us;
    grant faith, that we may be undeterred in our tasks;
    grant courage, as we face today and tomorrow with
        confidence;
    grant wisdom and guidance as we think through the life of
        the church;
that the thanksgiving we now offer and the fellowship we now
experience may inspire us to new heights of praise and
service.

142 Eternal God, by the power released into human life in Jesus,
you have pursued us down the years of our life and you will
not let us go. We have tried so often to close our ears to your
voice, to shut the doors of our mind, but still you come and
come again.

We have hidden behind pious phrases but you penetrate
their shallowness; we have lost ourselves in endless activity

but you make us pause in our headlong rush and think again; we have chatted our way through the 'ifs and buts' of idle speculation about the faith but you have silenced us and made us listen; you have burst into our noisy lives and crept into our silence.

And we are glad. Glad that you disturb us; glad that you persist in your searching; glad that you come upon us unawares to confront us with your presence. For, as our wills have bowed to yours, as your persistent word has challenged us, as you have called us to love, to compassion and to service, we have found life, a life that endures and is stronger than death.

143 Father, we thank you that within the family of the church we find friendship. We are grateful for the support and goodwill of Christian friends around us. This is part of the joy of belonging to the church family.
The comfort, peace and love of Christian friendship give us strength. As we find these joys in our own lives may we also give them. Help us to love and serve each other so that our thankfulness is expressed in deed as well as word.

144 We praise and thank you, our Father, that as we become new creatures in Christ so we become eternally bound to each other.

We acknowledge with reverence the miracle of this new creation: your Church, the Body of Christ. We try to count all the blessings we have received from you and find that the greatest is that you have chosen us to be part of your Body on earth. Such knowledge is too wonderful for us, yet we ask that we may respond to the unbelievable trust you have placed in us by being more ready to serve you with our whole being.

We remember that all who acknowledge Christ as the source of their newness of life are part of his Body with us.

Grant, O living Christ, that we may work together in unity
and love, seeking only what will enhance the beauty of your
Church and its effective showing forth of your love. So may
more and more people be incorporated into the mystical
Body, that your name may be glorified.

145   To the prayer: *We thank you, Father God,* the response is:
For giving us each other.

Let us offer thanks for the rich variety of God's gifts among
his people.

Remembering the energy of youth and the wisdom of age:
    We thank you, Father God: *For giving us each other.*
Remembering the different contribution that each member
makes out of his daily experience of life:
    We thank you, Father God: *For giving us each other.*
Remembering our fellow-Christians in other churches:
    We thank you, Father God: *For giving us each other.*
Remembering our growing unity with Christians all round
the world:
    We thank you, Father God: *For giving us each other.*
Remembering those who have influenced us in years gone by
and now worship you in heaven:
    We thank you, Father God: *For giving us each other.*
All praise to you, eternal God, for you have given us Jesus
Christ who has gathered us all together and holds us in your
love.
    We thank you, Father God: *For giving us each other.*

146   Following each part of the prayer the response is: *We thank
you, Lord.*

For the fun of outings:
    We thank you, Lord.
For the eager looking-forward, counting the days and
counting the hours:
    We thank you, Lord.

For the longed-for day's beginning, early call and special clothes, hurried breakfast, shouting send-off:
We thank you, Lord.
For the the happiness of travelling with people we know, for the thrills, the unexpected, the jokes along the way:
We thank you, Lord.
For the fellowship, for the food eaten, shared and enjoyed with our special friends around us:
We thank you, Lord.
For the singing, homeward way, ending with the lights of home:
We thank you, Lord.
For the fun of outings:
We thank you, Lord.

147   We who are grown up thank you, Lord, for children; for their trust and dependence; for their sense of wonder; for their insight into truth which has escaped us; for their sheer enjoyment of living. As once you set a child in the midst, not to be taught but to teach, give us humility to do the same.

148   We who are young thank you, Lord, for grown-up people; for their answers to our questions; for the help they give us in trouble and difficulty; for showing us how to do so many things; for teaching us about the Christian faith. Help us to show our gratitude by being welcoming and helpful to older people.

149   In the quietness, let us think for a moment of Christians who have served in the Church, and the world, and who have now died.

We thank you, God, for all those who have heard the call of
Jesus, and have responded with their lives.
We thank you for the first disciples; for those who have
served the kingdom through the years; for those who have
served in this church, and shared their faith with us. In
silence we name before you those who have served us in
special ways, influencing our lives and leading us to faith.
   Silence
We know that they still serve the same kingdom with us, and
that we belong together in Christ. As we learn from their
successes and failures so may we offer ourselves as servants
of your kingdom.

150   Thanksgiving and praise to you, Lord Jesus Christ.
Thank you for the gifts you have already given us today; for
all we have seen, heard and received in home and church,
town and world.
Thank you for our friends. Thank you for our life together in
the church. Thank you for a day quieter than most. Thank
you for the opportunity to worship.

In your name, Lord Jesus Christ, we each silently recall, with
thanksgiving:
   a sight we have seen today that pleased us;
      Silence
   a sound we have heard today that delighted us;
      Silence
   a person we have met today who gave us pleasure;
      Silence
   a truth that has dawned on us afresh today.
      Silence

Thank you for life. Thank you for grace. Thank you for
being present in our day; for taking us seriously as individual
people with personal needs, hopes and fears. Thank you for
gathering our gifts of worship into your hands to offer to your
Father, who you tell us is our Father as well.
Thank you, Lord.

151   Almighty God, open wide our hearts that we may welcome
the stranger and share our faith with others; open wide our
minds that we may receive new truth and understand your
will; open wide our doors that as we have come in to worship
so we may go out with you to the service of the world; open
wide our lives that through discipline and prayer we may
experience your power in daily living.

152   Eternal God, origin of all creation, your Spirit has led
mankind in the search for truth and the growth of
compassion. Since you are the Father of us all, let your Spirit
enter our hearts with gentle strength to give us true unity.

Unite us in our rejection of all that mars your creation and in
the furtherance of all that enriches life. Help us to stand
alongside each other in both joy and grief so that we find
common purpose in our free search for all that is truly
valuable in human life.

Acknowledging our human frailty, we rely on your protection
and love. We submit to your purposes, seeking only to serve
you so that your goal becomes our goal, and our human
triumphs are taken up into the victory of your Son.

(Based on the hymn 'Eternal Ruler of the ceaseless round')

153   The life we share as disciples of Jesus Christ is so much more
than the following of a rule book or the words of his
teaching: it is the experience of life itself lived with Jesus and
with each other.

Father, it is this sense of belonging to Jesus and to each other
that gives us courage in our discipleship, strength in
moments of weakness, and comfort in times of loneliness.
We rejoice in our fellowship together and ask for your love in
building up our trust in one another, our sharing and caring,
that we may truly show we are the friends of Jesus.

154 *Pre-school children*

Lord Jesus Christ, who enjoyed the happiness and security of
a home in Nazareth, and who later gave your love and
blessing to boys and girls, we remember today our very young
ones, and ask that you will hold them in your love. May they,
through the good influence of their parents and families and
of your church, learn to grow up, as you did, in wisdom and
favour with God and men. Help them in the days of
dependency to learn how to share with others, and so be
ready to take their place in school and in the world.

155 *The care of children*

Father God, we pray for the children and young people of
our church, and for those who are beginning to sense the
wonder, the mystery, and the difficulty of life. They are part
of this church family which you have brought together in
fellowship and care. We pray for understanding and wisdom
in our worship and life together, so that all we do may lead
our children into a fuller and richer understanding of your
love and purpose. Help us to respond to their needs. Give us
patience and compassion. Help us to offer them our time and
our experience with true sincerity and love.

Workers with children in church

156 We thank you, Lord, for those who have accepted the care
and leadership of children and young people in the church.
May your Holy Spirit increase in them the gifts and skills
they bring to their work; grant them patience, imagination
and love sufficient for their tasks and, in the fullness of time,
crown their service with true success.

157 Eternal God, in Jesus we see love set before us in a way that
can never fully be copied by us, yet standing as a constant

hope and challenge in our struggle to love. In him we see the fulfilment of our strivings after compassion. We pray that love may increase, and it is this hope that brings us to church.

Look at us, O God, in our family life: husband with wife, parents with children, friend with friend. Let love be strong enough to bring us to maturity in our relationships.

Look at us as we live alone, separated from loved ones by bereavement, or in a solitariness chosen or enforced. Let our inner resources of love be strong enough to withstand isolation or loneliness.

Look at us in the daily life of the world as we seek to create a new society. Help us to love and by our love to transform the unlovely. Inspire us to use our power and influence in releasing the resources of society for those who are weak and underprivileged.

Look at us in the life of the church. Let love hold us together in the swirl of change. Let love provide so secure a foundation that we can allow Christian disagreement. Let love be the bond of our conversation, the power behind our search for your will, and the springboard of our service to others. Let love be in our worship so that we hold hands in a circle of praise and adoration.

In the name of him who came amongst us with love unconditional and everlasting, even Jesus Christ our Lord.

158   God, our Father, so much of the faith is in discovering through all our lives the wonder of your love and purpose for mankind: the richness and majesty of your creative and providing love, the way you have guided men through the centuries, the supreme picture of your love in Jesus Christ, your call to us in our own day.

We pray for all who share in unfolding this picture to us: for ministers and preachers who enlarge and enrich our understanding of God, and help us to respond to his love; for all who work among children and young people in our church, not only imparting knowledge but, by their lives, example and faith, sharing in moulding young lives; for those involved in house fellowships or study groups, and all who seek maturity in their understanding of the faith; for the whole family of God that we, both old and young, may reach towards a rich understanding of God, and live with a child-like dependence upon his love.

159   Father of us all, we rejoice in the church into which you have called us. We pray for our children and young people, that they may be granted deepening insight into the meaning of life; for those offering service, that their abilities may be wisely used; for the elderly, that faith may ever grow stronger; and for those who are ill, that they may discover inner resources of strength. May your church be strong in all that is good and thus serve your purpose.

160   Lord God, you are the Father of all people and we bring our prayers knowing that you will hear us and help us.

We pray for the whole family of your church. Grant that we, and all your people, may be built up in our faith, and always show in our lives the love we see in Jesus. Give courage to those who find it hard to follow you; to those who are finding it difficult to have faith because of a personal hardship or tragedy; to those who are made to suffer for their faith. Let your Holy Spirit support them, and may all Christians stand firm in the hope that your kingdom of love will come in all the world.

We pray for our country. Let your love surround the Queen and her family; give wisdom and guidance to our statesmen and leaders, and to all who have responsibility in education, in industry and in commerce.

We pray for people who are ill, those who are sad and those

who are hurt in any way. We pray especially for those known
to us in this church. Let your love surround them and give
them your peace.

We pray for one another. Help us to grow together in faith
and love, rejoicing in your fatherhood and that we can bring
our prayers to you in the name of Jesus Christ.

161   What's that you say, Lord?
    Send your grain overseas, and in time you will get a return.
    You love a cheerful giver.
    You accept what a man has, not asking for what he has
       not.
    Sparse sowing, sparse reaping!
But we like to hold on to what we have.
We go on the defensive when giving is mentioned.
Generosity is costly.
Yet we know that it is right, for when a man has more than
    enough, his wealth does not give him life.

So, Lord, come and put a new spirit into our hearts.
Make us glad to give; eager to serve; keen to sacrifice.
Let the joy of a needy person helped,
    the relief of resources used,
    the power of a strong church equipped to serve,
be our reward.

162   Lord God, we bring gifts.

We bring the past as a gift to you:
    the experience it has given us:
    its successes and failures, its wisdom and folly,
    its hurt and its remembered joy;
and with the past we bring our prayer that we may use it to
understand ourselves, the people around us, and our part in
the life of the world, thus enriching the work we do in your
name.

We bring the present as a gift to you:
    this fleeting moment slipping through our minds,
    this day in which we worship and reflect on life,
    this opportunity to understand and be understood,
    this church which serves and worships in the present
       moment;
and with the present we bring the prayer that we may be
sensitive to your presence within it, and be thus enabled to
make it a thank-offering of love.

We bring the future to you:
    it is uncertainly ours yet still it is our gift to you,
    it is unknown yet still we believe we can offer it in Christ's
       name;
and with the future we bring our visions and hopes for it, our
fear and apprehension, in the confidence that, living in the
eternal now, you will be our God.

Lord God, we bring gifts: the past, the present and the
future. And yet how can we? They are already yours; your
gifts to us. Show us rather how to use what you have given,
rejoice in what you are giving, and trust you for what we are
yet to receive.

Offertory

163   Heavenly Father, you have given us life and family, home
and friends. These good things are your gifts to us. We thank
you for them all. We thank you especially for Jesus our Lord.
Through him we know you, we know your love and care for
us. We seek to follow him. Fill our hearts with thankfulness
till they overflow. We want to love you, Father, with our
whole being. That is why we bring our gifts to you. Give us
wisdom to use them well so that your will may be done.

164   We admit, Lord, that we have frequently offered our gifts
without care and without preparation; that money set aside

for the offertory has been an afterthought instead of a first-fruit; that we have spent more on luxuries than on gifts such as these. Forgive us if these gifts are less than our best, use them to your glory, and make us better stewards of the bounty that is ours.

165   Deliver us, O Lord, from thinking of ourselves more highly than we ought. Since every virtue we possess is yours alone, may we use humbly such gifts as we have, thankful to be of service for your sake.

166   Lord, when you saw the widow putting her mite in the box, you knew she had given everything out of love. When we give our money or our time to your church remind us that it means nothing unless we also give our hearts and try to serve you always.

167   Lord, with our gifts we show our love. We love you because you first loved us. So our giving is full of joy because you have given us a gift we could never deserve in Jesus Christ our Lord.

At the close of worship

168   Lord, may your peace surround us, your love enrich us, and your presence encourage us, this day and for evermore.

169   Strengthen us and use us, O Lord; fashion us again in your own image; send us to dare and to do great things for you, that men may know again your love and your power.

LIFE AND MISSION

170   Lord God, you made people to worship you and shout aloud your glory. How wonderful it is that people in every land are meeting to worship you!

Before our day has begun, your people in eastern lands are already praising you. Long after our day has ended, your people in the west are meeting to pray and praise. In each place your people worship you in the way they know and love. They speak to you in their own language and know that you understand.

Lord God, you made people to worship you and shout aloud your glory. How wonderful it is that people in every land are meeting to worship you!

171   God of all nations, Father of all men, forgive us for our greed and complacency in a world where your gifts are so badly divided:
we load our trolleys in the supermarket whilst others huddle
    over a bowl of rice;
we build our second garages whilst millions live in shacks;
we choose carelessly from the stacked bookshelves whilst
    many of the new literates have nothing to read;
we sweat over our Gross National Product whilst most are
    concerned with minimum survival standards.

Father, forgive us! Empower those who work for fairer sharing, and give to all of us a keener conscience that this injustice may be righted and all your children be provided with the means to live as your children should.

172   O God our Father, as we pray for your blessing to rest upon the Church, it is the church here in this place which comes most naturally to our minds. We are grateful for its worship and fellowship; for the care and teaching of children and young people; for its nurture and love. Help us to see the kind of church you need today, Lord. May we not lose sight of the many and varied needs of this neighbourhood. Hold up before us the vision of your kingdom, a kingdom of justice and mercy, truth and compassion. Help us to grasp the meaning of the gospel which you have entrusted to us, and give us grace to live by it.

173 O God our Father, because we are part of your family, we know that you have given us a job to do of telling our friends and other people about the Lord Jesus.

Very often we find it difficult because we don't know the words to say, or when to say them, and we ask for the help of your Holy Spirit as we try to witness for you.

Thank you, God our Father, for letting us share your work.

174 Eternal God, we are conscious of the responsibility you have given your Church to be your people in the world. We are conscious also that your Church must live in different situations.

Where it is set in the midst of affluence, may it exhibit the true values of your kingdom.
Where it is surrounded by poverty, may it be ready to minister to the needs of men and women.
Where it is set in the face of war, may it act as peacemaker.
Where it encounters apathy, may it be able to excite people to action.
Where it is facing injustice, may it proclaim true right-eousness.

We pray for the power of your Spirit to enable your Church to fulfil its mission in every situation.

175   We thank you, O Lord, that in a world where many
disagreements exist between men and nations, your gospel
comes to break down the barriers that divide, bringing
friendship that extends across all boundaries because of our
common faith in Jesus Christ.

We pray today for your church in lands other than our own:
in countries where governments are hostile to Christianity
give your people courage and endurance in the face of
opposition;
in nations where other religions hold sway give your people
wisdom, patience and love.

Father, we thank you for the new insights into the meaning
of the gospel that are coming from many parts of the world.
Make us more ready to listen to what your people in other
lands have to say to us, and help us all to share and work
together for the unity of all men and the coming of your
kingdom.

176   *Into all the world*

Lord God, you call us to share in your mission to all the
world. You have given the gospel of Jesus for all people and
we must share his gospel with everyone.

Strengthen us to serve you in the places where we live and
work, that our deeds and actions may show to others that we
are your people and follow in the way of Jesus Christ.

Help us to play our part in the life of the Church throughout
the world, by our prayers for all Christian people, and by our
gifts of money and of service.

May your people, in every land and of every race, show to the
world that the gospel of Jesus can break down all the barriers
that divide, and that all people are equally your children,
belonging together and sharing in the joy of your kingdom.

177 *Christians in other lands*

God of all people, we are glad that the family of your Church
stretches out all over the world. We pray for your blessing to
be upon our Christian brothers and sisters in other lands.
Where they are a small minority let them find strength in
knowing you are with them; where they are persecuted let
them find courage to continue faithful, knowing that you
will never leave them; where they are young in the faith let
your Holy Spirit build them up in the knowledge of your love;
where they are affluent and accepted keep them constant in
the service of Jesus.

Father, we praise you that we are bound together in Jesus
Christ to all those who love and serve him. As we are blessed
by the prayers of others, may our prayer be a blessing to
those who love and worship you in other lands, through Jesus
Christ, the head over all the Church.

Serving

178 Thank you, Father, for the work of Christian Aid:
  for the help given to millions of people in their distress or
    hardship, or their struggle for a more human life;
  for the energy and vision of Christians overseas who take
    what we give and use it with justice and love;
  for the energy and vision of all who persevere in their work
    for world development, by giving, by praying, by the
    search for understanding and the plea for changes that
    serve justice and peace.

179 God, our Creator and Father, whose Son Jesus Christ
commanded us to love one another, and said that what we do
for people in need is service rendered unto him: we confess
that our lives are so unlike his, and that we conveniently
ignore his command, going thoughtlessly on as though

poverty and hunger did not exist. By our failure to love we bring shame on you. Father, forgive us.

God, our Creator and Father, thank you for furnishing this world with rich resources. Thank you for the wealth of land and sea, for skills of mind and hand. Thank you for the dedication of those who give their time and talents for the benefit of others, for workers in relief organisations who serve in your name.

God, our Creator and Father, we pray for those who are weary with the relentless struggle to keep alive; for those who can never look forward to a good meal and a comfortable bed, and who barely have the necessities of life, much less its extras. We seek the removal of all that prevents a fully human life in others.

God, our Creator and Father, teach us the meaning of true love; make us so open to the influence of Jesus that we give and serve to the point of sacrifice, and so bring hope to those in despair.

180 *Caring*

God our Father, we pray:
  for people who are hungry while we have enough;
  for people who have too little because we have too much;
  for people in other lands who, like us, live and laugh, love
    their children and work for their future.

Help us to give with respect that we may one day receive with thanksgiving.

For refugees

181 Father, you care for all your children. We know it must hurt you to see some of your children suffering and dying from lack of shelter and food, whilst others have more than enough. We pray today for those who are without homes and especially those who have been forced to flee their home country. We remember that Jesus was born in a stable and had to be taken to a foreign land. We ask that your love may surround all refugees today. Through the concern of your people and the action of relief agencies and governments, we ask that their problems may be overcome and a new way of life opened to them.

182 Seeking a refuge, seeking a home, seeking love and under-standing and friendship — hundreds and thousands of them: we call them refugees. All of them victims of war, disease, natural disaster or hopelessness. Lord, we feel helpless in the face of such need. They don't knock on our door: we see them on television news and documentaries, but we see pictures like theirs every week, and we've grown hardened. Soften our hearts, Lord, that we may work for a world where hunger, exploitation, ignorance and violence will be ended. We pray for the ways in which governments and voluntary agencies can help. Give to each of us such a concern for our fellow-man that our complacency is shattered and we give all that is required of us in sacrifice and service.

For developing countries

183 We pray, O Father, for developing countries. May their leaders work for the good of all people and may prejudice against new things not impede their growth. Strengthen those who seek to help them. May the nations of the world be prepared to sacrifice in the service of others and be given patience and love to lead them into fullness of life.

184 What a world, Lord! But it is the world we have inherited. One-third is rich, and two-thirds are poor, and the gap is getting wider.

Lord God, help the Third World to know that there are many people determined to gain justice for them; determined to change the pattern of trade and finance so that they get a fair deal.

Grant your wisdom and your strength, Lord, to those who speak and act in the name of the Church that there may be justice for all peoples in all the earth.

SPECIAL OCCASIONS

New year

185 Let us recall those men of faith through whom God promised his loving care to his people, and let us learn from their experience.

We think of Noah who was called to make a new beginning:
O God, forgive our past failures and our share in the wickedness of the world. As a new year dawns give us grace to make a new beginning in your service.

We think of Abraham who was called to leave the familiar and venture into the unknown:
O God, give us courage to face whatever the coming year may bring, knowing that nothing can separate us from your love in Jesus Christ.

We think of Moses who was guided in the wilderness:
O God, whether the way ahead is rough or smooth make us sensitive to every sign of your presence and guidance.

We think, most of all, of Jesus who was called to sacrifice himself, in life and in death, for the salvation of the world:
O God, we hear your call to follow in the footsteps of Christ. Take all we have and are and, whatever the cost, help us to live and die to your glory.

186 A whole new year is waiting for us, each day untouched and
unspoiled and full of opportunity; each day a gift from God,
like life itself, given to us to make of it what we can. Here
and now is the opportunity to resolve to live each day to
God's glory and purpose.

And so we renew our promises before God in new year
resolution, not made in fun for quick forgetting, but
made in holy love — God's love to us and our response. God
loved the world so much as to give his only Son that we might
have life — and it is our lives we offer to him to make the very
best of them.

Lord, take our lives and the vows we make today that we may
be children worthy of the name Christian, living to your glory
day by day.

187 *Week of prayer for Christian unity*

Lord, you are one: one Lord, one Father, and you call us to
be one people and one family.

We are sorry for the many times when we do not behave like
your family. Father, forgive us:
    for our pride when we want to do your work on our own;
    for our lack of vision when we are unable to see beyond our
      own little church;
    for our fear when we prefer the safety of our familiar
      habits;
    for our hypocrisy when we proclaim that we belong to-
      gether but fail to love each other and act in close family
      spirit;
    for our unfaithfulness to you when we forget our brothers
      and sisters.

Help us, Lord, to grow together in Christian unity, to learn
to love each other so that we might be a closer family for your
sake.

Unity of the Church

188 Lord God, we give you thanks for the unity we can see within
your Church:
> for our one Master, Jesus Christ, whose name we take and
> who calls us to be his disciples;
> for the Bible which opens to us your ways with men and
> women;
> for the gospel ordinances of baptism and the Lord's
> Supper;
> for our common heritage of worship on Sunday, the day of
> resurrection;
> and for our one task of showing your love for all people in
> all the world.

We give thanks for the breaking down of barriers that have
divided the churches through the centuries;
> for the sharing of worship;
> for the sharing in service and help to people in need;
> for the coming together of different denominations;
> and for the recognition that we all belong to the one
> Father.

We give thanks that your Holy Spirit is calling us to express
our oneness in Christ in new ways, and that he will not let us
rest until we are truly one people of God, to the glory of your
holy name.

189 Lord Jesus, we pray for the unity of your Church.

Give us grace to break down any barriers that still divide us
from our fellow-Christians; strengthen the witness we make
together in this town, and open our minds and hearts to the
Holy Spirit that we may join more fully in the common
mission you have given to your Church.

Keep us active in seeking that fuller unity for which you
prayed, that we may be one even as you and the Father are
one. We ask this for your name's sake.

Mothering Sunday

190 God our Father, all through our lives we have reason to be thankful for our mothers.

When we are babies they do everything for us and spend much of their time feeding us and keeping us warm and clean.

When we are children they teach us, help and comfort us, sharing our hobbies and our ideas and keeping us happy.

When we marry and have families of our own, they still support us, advise us and share our troubles and joys.

When they grow old themselves they still love and care about us, though they may be weak and tired.

We are better people because of all they have done for us.

We thank you, O God, for our mothers and pray that the love they show may also be shown by us.

191 Lord Jesus Christ, we are glad that the Bible story tells us a little about your family life and introduces us to Mary, your mother.

   She was thrilled and happy when she knew she was to be a
      mother.
   She went through pain and discomfort so that you could
      be born.
   She was pleased when people were glad to meet you.
   She was worried when you were lost, and she went to look
      for you.
   She was concerned when she thought you were working too
      hard.
   She stayed by you when everyone else was against you.
   She shared your pain and suffering and she shared your
      triumph.

Because in the love of our own mothers we also have received this same care, we give God thanks and praise.

192 *Church anniversary*

On this happy day, we thank you, heavenly Father, for our
church here in ... . We praise you for all the joy we have
known in this church family; for our friends here; for leaders
and helpers; for those who plan and those who care, so that
our church may be a real home for all who share its life.

We thank you for the vision of the men and women who
worked and gave so that the church could be built, and we
thank you for all the loving sacrifice which has been shared
over the years.

Help us to realise that we are one with all Christians, no
matter which church they attend, and help us to remember
also that we are called to show the world the joy and fullness
of life which can be found only in Jesus Christ.

Grant that our church may be a blessing to all in this neighbourhood, so that more and more people may come to love
and trust you.

193 *Young people's service*

O God, we rejoice before you in the strength of our youth, for
it is your gift to us. We make it now our gift to you.

We thank you for our growing powers, and present them to
you now. Direct their development so that they are not
fruitless.

We thank you for life, open before us with all its range of
possibilities. Guide us in every choice we make so that we
travel your broad highway rather than choose cul-de-sacs of
our own making.

We thank you for our visions, knowing that they shape our
future. May they be true to your vision for us so that we do
not miss the goal of life.

Harvest

194 To the acclamation: *O Lord our Sovereign,* the response is:
How glorious is your name in the whole universe!

Sun, moon and planets sing your praise.
The vast silences of space are full of your glory.
    O Lord our Sovereign:
    How glorious is your name in the whole universe!
The earth is full of your riches.
Seedtime and harvest are in your hands.
Man works with you to provide his food.
    O Lord our Sovereign:
    How glorious is your name in the whole universe!
You have made man master over all your creatures.
His wisdom increases the fertility of the soil.
His wisdom must share it fairly among all.
    O Lord our Sovereign:
    How glorious is your name in the whole universe!
Teach man to be master also over himself,
that we may with sincerity proclaim:
    O Lord our Sovereign:
    How glorious is your name in the whole universe!

195 Great Lord and Maker of all things, stars and galaxies,
unbounded time and space, our minds explode with wonder
when we try to fathom your universe. Shall we ever plumb its
depths or understand its mysteries? Have you made us alone,
or as one of many planets peopled with life? Can we see your
purpose for this planet, beautiful earth, covered with sea and
clouds? Our questions show our wonder, and speak our
praise. Let everything in us praise you, now and for ever.

196 At the end of each section the response is: *Father, we give
thanks.*

We thank you, Father, for the life-giving quality of food.

It helps us to grow, it gives us energy, it clears the mind.
We thank you, Father, for the way you provide for our needs:
Father, we give thanks.

We thank you, Father, for the pleasures of food and drink;
for our favourite dish; for all the tastes and smells that make
our mouths water; for the satisfying feeling after a good
meal. We worship you, Father, by accepting your gifts with
thankfulness:
Father, we give thanks.

We thank you, Father, that, just as you supply the needs of
our bodies, you also feed our souls. Jesus is the bread of life.
He is the food for our souls. We feed on him, the Living
Bread:
Father, we give thanks.

197 We celebrate your creative power, O God. All that you have
made delights our senses: in touch and smell, in sight, sound
and taste.

Thank you for the harvest smells of fragrant flowers,
 for the harvest touch of polished fruits,
 for the harvest sights of overflowing goodness,
 for the harvest sounds of crunchy apples, the bite of
  carrots, and the rustle of golden corn,
 and for the wholesome taste that harvest gives through
  long winter months.

All that you have made delights us. May we use our creative
powers to produce that which delights and never that which
hurts. May we create beauty and not ugliness so that all we
are and all we make praises you, the Giver of all.

198 O Lord, how good it is to drink when we are thirsty; how
pleasant to let cool water trickle down our throats when we
are hot and parched; how comforting to sip a steaming hot

drink when we are cold or wet. We think of the many kinds
of drink — fruit juices, squashes, ice-cream sodas, milk, tea,
coffee, cocoa, chocolate, bedtime drinks — and we thank
you for them all.

We thank you, Lord, for the great variety of plants which you
have caused to grow upon the earth and from which we
obtain the ingredients for our drinks. You are a great and
mighty Creator, and we praise you.

199   Lord God, when you made the world you saw that it was
very good. But you left the fulfilling of your work to
mankind, giving him dominion over all the works of your
hands.

By your wisdom we have done many wonderful things:
> you have enabled us to conquer distance and bring people
> closer to each other;
> you have enabled us to flourish and grow rich;
> you have given us enlarged opportunities for education
> and varied work by which we earn our living;
and we give thanks and praise.

But in the midst of our thankful praise we remember that
there are many hungry people; some still struggle to help
themselves, and others have reached the point where the
struggle is no longer worthwhile; some are hindered
because we cannot understand their needs, and others are
made worse because their needs conflict with ours.

Lord, as this day we give thanks for our daily bread, we link
ourselves in prayer, hope and love with this hungry,
frightened world.

200   Yet again, O God, by the miracle of your eternal providence
seed-time has brought forth harvest. Teach us, O Lord, to
reverence the earth which you make fruitful. Keep us
mindful at this time of those who sow the seed and reap the
harvest. Fill us with compassion for those who have not

enough to eat. Having shared with us something of your
wisdom whereby the earth can produce enough and to spare,
inspire us again with the spirit of Jesus so that those who
have may readily share with those who have not.

201   Following each part of the prayer the response is: *We pray
for your blessing, O Lord.*

Lord God, you have created the earth and given to us gifts
for our use.

On the earth and all that is in it,
on the harvest of the soil,
on the trade and industry of the people,
and on the work whereby we obtain your gifts:
   We pray for your blessing, O Lord.

On those who search for your treasures hidden in the earth,
on those who labour to make them fit for our use,
on craftsmen and manufacturers,
on architects and builders,
and on engineers and planners:
   We pray for your blessing, O Lord.

On merchants and traders who bring goods from other
      lands,
on those who go to sea in ships,
on those who fly,
and on those who work in docks and harbours and airports:
   We pray for your blessing, O Lord.

On all who trade with us in the shop or in the market,
on all who serve at the counter or in the office,
on those who make available what we need for life, for
      comfort and enjoyment:
   We pray for your blessing, O Lord.

Lord God, you have given to us so many gifts. May we not
selfishly hoard them, nor foolishly squander them, but care
for all mankind, and share what you have given us; through
Jesus Christ our Lord.

Remembrance Sunday

202 To the prayer: *Father, forgive us our sins,* the response is:
As we forgive those who sin against us.

Father, today we remember the horrors of war, past and
present. We remember the killing and the grief, the
wounding and the destruction, the suffering of innocent and
guilty, the cries of men, women and children.

Forgive the evil in us that makes war possible.

If we have wanted more than we need, and tried to take it
from others, Father, forgive us our sins:
As we forgive those who sin against us.

If we have been jealous of other people's happiness or
success, Father, forgive us our sins:
As we forgive those who sin against us.
If we have looked down on people who are different from
us because of their accent, their education, their work,
their clothes and appearance, or the colour of their skin,
Father, forgive us our sins:
As we forgive those who sin against us.

If we have let our minds and hearts become deadened to the
suffering of people far away, Father, forgive us our sins:
As we forgive those who sin against us.

Father, give us such love for others that we are not simply
peaceful people wanting no trouble, but peacemakers, able
and willing to walk humbly, to act justly, and to love.

203 To the versicle: *For all men of peace,* the response is: *Thank
you, Prince of peace.*

Lord Jesus Christ, you said, 'How blest are the peacemakers;
God shall call them his sons.' Today we give thanks for those
who seek to make peace in this divided world.

For the Secretary General and the staff of the United Nations
Organisation, and for those who are prepared to work long
hours of travel to any country in the cause of peace:
> For all men of peace: *We thank you, Prince of peace.*

For governments who are prepared to send units for the
difficult rôle of a peace-keeping force:
> For all men of peace: *We thank you, Prince of peace.*

For those who work to bring together opposing sides in
disputes between management and men, and for all who act
as arbitrators in difficult situations:
> For all men of peace: *We thank you, Prince of peace.*

For Christians and non-Christians who quietly and stead-
fastly advocate and live in the way of peace, and thereby
work for its growth:
> For all men of peace: *We thank you, Prince of peace.*

For those who are willing to risk their lives in the trouble-
spots of the world in order to build bridges of understanding
between peoples of different races and colour:
> For all men of peace: *We thank you, Prince of peace.*

For people like ourselves who, having known the bitterness
which hatred and strife can create in families and between
individuals, seek in your strength to sow seeds of peace:
> For all men of peace: *We thank you, Prince of peace.*

Count us, Lord Christ, among those who are peacemakers,
that we may be children of our heavenly Father.

204 Lord, you look on man making war, killing, wasting your
gifts, and it grieves you. We pray for those parts of the world
where there is conflict. You sent your Son to reconcile man
to yourself and to his fellow-man; it is your purpose that all
might be brought into unity in Christ. So may the Spirit of
Christ rule in the hearts of men, that east and west, rich and
poor, black and white, may come together and find their
common life in him.

205   Jesus said, 'How blest are the peacemakers.'

We pray for all men and women who have the job of making peace in our world:
>   the leaders of nations who sit around a table and discuss ways of living together;
>   the diplomats of the world who are to be ambassadors of courtesy and understanding;
>   the men and women of the United Nations Organisation and its agencies which seek to bring men closer together in peace.

Jesus said, 'How blest are the peacemakers; God shall call them his sons.'

May all those who work for peace know your strength and encouragement which comes from the depths of peace Jesus promises us in his spirit.

206   *Bible Sunday*

To the affirmation: *God has spoken,* the response is: *Thanks be for the living word.*

In the authority of the Law, and in the discernment of the Prophets; in the wisdom of the Proverbs, and in the beauty of the Psalms:
>   God has spoken: *Thanks be for the living word.*

In the compelling truth of the Gospels, and the Letters which apply the truth to human situations; above all in Jesus, his Son, our Saviour, the Word made flesh:
>   God has spoken: *Thanks be for the living word.*

In our own language, through the scholarship and sacrifice of translators of the past, and in modern English, through men and women who have released God's voice for contemporary ears:
>   God has spoken: *Thanks be for the living word.*

In a thousand languages as the Bible societies have trans-

lated, published and distributed for the sake of millions newly able to read:
God has spoken: *Thanks be for the living word.*

In the need of our human condition; in the searching of our minds for spiritual truth; in the sorrow of our sinfulness:
God has spoken: *Thanks be for the living word.*

Infant baptism

207 O Lord, look in love and kindness upon all parents who care for a young baby. Give them wisdom in their new-found responsibility. Grant that they may set an example of love and goodness in their lives, and may your Holy Spirit of joy abide in their hearts and home.

208 Lord, you called Jesus into your service at his baptism in Galilee. (*Name*) has just been baptised and we rejoice together in welcoming *him* in your name. But let this service be more than a church welcome; by the power of your Spirit, call *him* and *his* parents to be disciples of Jesus so that (*name*) may grow as one of your faithful children.

May *he* grow to know you as *his* friend and the inspiration of *his* life and may *his* loving response to you be seen in *his* life.

Father God, this is what we wish for (*name*) now and in days to come. Help us to do our part in making this wish come true by our loving, teaching and caring for *him* in your name.

209 *Adult baptism*

Lord, you called Jesus into your service at his baptism in Galilee. (*Name*) has just been baptised and we rejoice together

in welcoming *him* in your name. But let this service be more
than a church welcome; by the power of your Spirit renew your
call to (*name*) to be a disciple of Jesus, so that *he* may continue
and develop as a faithful member of your family. May *he* know
you continually as *his* friend and the inspiration of *his* life and
may *his* loving response to you be seen in his life of faith.

Father God, this is what we wish for (*name*) now and in days to
come. Help us to do our part in making this wish come true by
supporting *him* and sharing our discipleship in Christ.

210   *Dedication of a child*

Lord Jesus, we are glad that you welcomed children and gave
them your blessing. In your name we have dedicated (*name*) to
you and acknowledged that *he* is your child. Surround *him*
with gifts of the Holy Spirit, that *he* may grow up in faith and
be found your faithful soldier and servant all *his* days.

We thank you for *his* parents, and especially that they have
brought (*name*) to be dedicated to you. Bless their home and
give them wisdom and love as they bring up (*name*) as a
Christian child.

We pray for your church, that children may be nurtured in
the family of faith, and that in all our words and deeds we
may set forth Jesus Christ as the way, the truth and the life.
Grant that we do nothing which will hurt one of your
children but that in them we may see you, and in ministering
to them find that we are ministering to you. For your name's
sake.

211   *Promotion time*

Lord Jesus, you are with us through every period of our life.
As we grow up may we continue in your love and service.

Bless the children who are growing up within this church family. May they find the true spirit of discipleship in our worship and our work together. Be with them in every new experience this day and through all their days.

Opening prayer at Holy Communion
when children are present

212   We are your family, Lord, and we have come to your table because you invite us. We know that you join with us because you promised your disciples that you would always be with them. Hear us today, in the prayers we shall say, in the praises we shall bring, in the thanksgiving for all your gifts, and in the offering of ourselves. Then feed us, Lord, in your own way with bread and wine as you did the first disciples. In this way we shall be renewed as your people, your followers, your new disciples.

213   We are here, Lord, because you said, 'Do this in remembrance of me.' We are here, Lord, to repeat your words, and to take bread and wine as you took them long ago. When we do these things and say these words we are joining with our Christian friends all round the world, and back through time to the first of your friends in the upper room. And we join ourselves to you because this is your meal, at your table, in your house, and you have invited us. Thank you for letting us be here. Accept all we say and do in this service, and take us for yourself, now and always.

Part 3
General Prayers

DISCOVERING GOD'S WORLD

New discoveries

214 Father, thank you for the thrill of finding something new;
thank you for the joy of discovering something we didn't
know before; thank you for the discoveries we make about
life, about love, about ourselves; thank you for other people's
new ideas, and for all the inventions that add something
good to living.

215 After each part of the prayer the response is: *We give thanks
to Almighty God, revealed in Jesus the Christ.*

For creation around us:
    mighty seas and rolling plains,
    tiny flowers and fields of beauty,
    useful food and needful drink,
    science and art;
    *We give thanks to Almighty God, revealed in Jesus the
    Christ.*

For our own creation:
    hand and eye in co-operation,
    mind intent and body active,
    learning, seeking, enquiring,
    knowledge passed through generations;
    *We give thanks to Almighty God, revealed in Jesus the
    Christ.*

For our new creation in Christ:
  gifts of Bible, Church and worship,
  spirits alert to God's presence,
  inner growth and outward signs of grace,
  love received and love restored;
  We give thanks to Almighty God, revealed in Jesus the Christ.

For the creation of the Church:
  a family uniting all ages,
  a family present in the broad sweep of history,
  a family keen to worship, eager to serve,
  a family of God;
  We give thanks to Almighty God, revealed in Jesus the Christ.

216 Lord, you are everywhere to be found. Your Spirit is active in all the world.

  We see you in the dynamic forces of continuing creation.
  We hear you in the conversation of friends, the arguments
    that reveal truth, and the debate among nations.
  You are present in laboratory and lecture room, in
    research, and all human thoughtfulness.
  Wherever a hand is offered in friendship, a voice speaks
    in welcome, or eyes reflect forgiveness, you are there.

Spirit of God, you work within and beyond our experience.
Here in worship we ask for your gifts.

Give us
  an awareness of your presence,
  sensitivity to respond to your promptings,
  virile liveliness to measure our actions to your guidance,
  and, above all, eyes unclouded by prejudice so that we may
    proclaim you Lord in every place where honest
    experience sees the evidence of your power.

Human creativity

217 We thank you, Father, the Creator, for making us creators like yourself. We thank you for the skills of men which have made a fuller life possible:
>   for printing presses which open the way to a world of
>   books and newspapers to stimulate our thinking;
>   for ships and cars, for rockets and planes which annihilate
>   time and space and compel us to come closer together;
>   for machines which build our homes, schools, hospitals
>   and roads;
>   for gadgets in our homes which make life easier;
>   for inventions which serve our leisure: radio and
>   television, tape-recorders and record-players;
>   for inventions which serve the sick and injured and
>   handicapped.

Father, you have given us skills, give us also the wisdom to use them wisely.

218 Almighty Father, you are not a selfish God. You do not keep the good things of your creation to yourself; you share them freely with us your children.

But more, you have shared with us your very power to create and make new. Therefore we thank you:
>   for the skill of fingers and hands,
>   for the gift of human imagination,
>   for the ability to co-ordinate hands and mind in one act
>   of creation,
>   for the patience which continues when creating is hard,
>   and for the persistence to begin again when things go
>   wrong.

Whilst we praise you for the ability to create the tangible things of life, we give you deeper thanks for the creative spirit working within us through our relationships:
>   for the ability to make friends,
>   for the gift of vital marriage relationships,

for caring family life,
and for the supportive community of the church.

As you have shared your creative gifts with us, O God, so
help us to share with others, using hand and eye, mind and
skill, friendship and love, for the good of others.

219   Father God, wonderful Creator, you have given to each one
of us talents and skills. Some of us are skilful at making
music or singing; some can read and speak clearly and well;
some are skilful with hands and fingers; some can paint, or
draw, or write beautifully; some can sew or knit or cook;
some are skilful at games and sports. Help each of us to
discover the skills you have given to us, to learn and train to
improve them, and then show us how we may use them to
serve you.

220   *Sense of touch*

We thank you, Father, for the joy that comes to us through
touching things. For the refreshing touch of water, the
smoothness of silk, the hardness of wood, and the handclasp
of a friend, we bring our gratitude to you. May we never take
your gifts for granted.

The world about us

221   To the affirmation:*The Lord, he is God,* the response is:
We glorify your holy name, O Lord.

Let us adore the might and majesty of God which we see
reflected in the wonder and mystery of his creation.

The wide places of the earth;
the vast expanse of space;
the limitless horizons of the sea, wonderful in its stillness
     and fearful in storm.

The Lord, he is God:
We glorify your holy name, O Lord.

The stretching polar icefields; the mystery of the voiceless
    deserts;
the minute wonders revealed by the microscope;
the perfection, the variety, the colour and the beauty
    manifest in all creation.
The Lord, he is God:
We glorify your holy name, O Lord.

The numerous peoples of the earth; the varieties of nation
    and race;
the wide-ranging differences of human hopes, culture,
    abilities and insights;
the God-given belief in brotherhood and tolerance glimpsed
    in the Church and seen best in Jesus.
The Lord, he is God:
We glorify your holy name, O Lord.

222   Thank you, Father God:
        for the warm summer weather, the shining sun,
        and the cold of the winter, snowballs and fun.

       Thank you, Father God:
        for summer sandcastles, the big splashing sea,
        and the fireside in winter with hot toast for tea.

       Thank you, Father God:
        for Sunday and worship, our praises to you,
        and for hymns, prayers and stories, old ones and new.

       Thank you, Father God:
        for service and caring, love given, received,
        and all who share with us a faith to believe.

       Thank you, Father God:
        for all that you give us, work-time and play,
        for summer and winter and every day.

223   Thank you, O God, for the expected things in life that never
fail:
for the day that always follows night;
for the seasons of the year, each in its own place;
for growth from seed to plant, plant to flower, and
flower to seed again;
for the love of families and the kindness of friends;
and for the promise that you will never leave us.

224   God, you have created a world full of colour, interest and
excitement, and we ask that you will help us always to go on
learning about life. Help us to discover more about other
people, so that we can serve them more lovingly. Help us to
discover more about the world, so that we can work with you
in making it a place where right values are honoured.

Lord, you are present in all people and in all life: as we
discover ourselves, others and the world, help us through all
our discoveries to discover you.

225   Lord, we come to you as men made blind: feeling our way
with faltering steps; prevented by the infirmity of our
humanity from knowing all there is to know and seeing all
there is to see.

Lord, open our eyes to ourselves,
to see with greater honesty our strengths and weaknesses,
to assess our abilities without pride or false modesty,
to acknowledge where faith falls short and admit it
without shame but rather in hope.
Help us to stand back from ourselves and so face up to what
we are.

Lord, open our eyes to each other, that we may learn
to accept each other with understanding,
to listen and talk with frankness,
to share agreement and disagreement in the spirit of love.

Help us to learn from each other's differing experiences of
life.

Lord, open our eyes to the world around us, through radio
and television, newspapers and conversations,
> to know with greater clarity the true needs of the world,
> to distinguish between the falsely sensational and the
> > truly dramatic news,
> to face up to features of life that disturb us.

Help us to sift the wheat from the chaff in the daily events of
life and to face tragedy and delight in the confidence that you
are in control.

Lord, above all else, open our eyes to the life of Jesus,
> the life he lived in the flesh and the life he now
> > lives in the power of the Spirit.
> Let his teaching pierce our complacency and our
> > prejudice.
> Let his life of love point to higher instincts within us.
> Let his death and rising be signposts to ultimate reality.

Lord, we are blind. Open our eyes and raise our sights to see
the splendour of your glory in the whole of life.

226 *Holidays*

Lord, we thank you for the refreshment which holiday brings
to our lives; for the excitement of anticipation and planning;
for the freedom from routine, and for new experiences and
opportunities. You have given us such a wonderful world
that wherever we go we are surrounded by things which
please our eyes and open our minds. Help us to use our
holidays to see your glory in creation. Help us to use our
freedom to understand more clearly the fullness of life you
are constantly offering us. Accept our thanks for the rich
variety of life which is your gift, and when our holidays are

over, help us to return to our homes safely with a new vision of your will for us.

227 *Space exploration*

Father, we thank you for the skill and invention of all who have shared in space exploration:
> the astronomers who search the skies with their telescopes and plot the course of stars and planets;
> the engineers and inventors who plan and build the space rockets;
> the astronauts who risk their lives to travel in space.

We praise you for the beauty and mystery of the heavens, for the secrets still hidden from us, and for the discoveries man has made. Help us not to be proud in our own achievements but humble before the immense power and range of the universe, for you are greater and more mysterious than anything we can ever discover. Long before we knew anything of space you had made yourself known to us in Jesus Christ, our Lord, and in his name we bring our thanksgiving.

CHRISTIAN LIFE-STYLE

228 Eternal God, you have given us freedom: freedom to work out the meaning and purpose of our own lives; freedom to accept or deny love, to accept or deny life, to accept you or deny you.
You, too, eternal God, are free: bound by no chains, limited by no lack of power, unrestrained in ability.
But we have seen you in action in the life of Jesus, when you denied your freedom to come to our aid. You bound the chains of love around your power; you shackled your strength with compassion and limited yourself to our advantage.
Help us to control our freedom by the love we also find within us.

229 O Lord, we have tried so hard to live better lives:
to be good-tempered and considerate;
to work hard instead of being lazy;
to watch our tongues and not speak hastily;
to be cheerful even when things go wrong;
to act kindly to people we find it hard to like.

But it is always the same story. Trying is not enough. Help us to catch your Spirit, through prayer and worship, fellowship and service, so that the fruit of the Spirit will grow in us, to your glory.

230 The fruit of the Spirit is love, joy, peace, patience, kindness, goodness, faithfulness, gentleness, self-control.

We admit with sorrow and shame, Lord Jesus, that we are often unloving and gloomy, quarrelsome and impatient; unkind and ill-natured; unreliable, harsh and self-indulgent.

How much we need the fruit of your Spirit! Grant us these qualities and help them to grow in us to your glory and for the good of others.

231 Lord Jesus, we find it easy to be angry. We are often angry over things which hurt us, and sometimes we even think we have the right to get our own back. But this is not your way. You taught us to forgive without counting the number of times we have been wronged. You showed by your example that we should never be quick to take offence. You were indignant only when people knowingly exploited others, saying they did it in the name of God; or when people knowingly traded on the fears and weaknesses of others. Even then you taught us to pray for wrongdoers.

Keep us so much in tune with your will that we speak out only against the things which are against God's will and purpose.

232   You have shown us how to forgive, Lord. In the story of the
prodigal son, the father did not hesitate to welcome back his
son, and he called others to rejoice with him; on the cross,
you befriended a thief; and after Peter had denied you, you
asked him to take responsibility for your people.

You have shown us how to forgive.
We remember in silence those who have done wrong to us.
   Silence
Help us to forgive them, Lord.
   Silence

Lord, we forgive them in your name and pray for mercy
ourselves.

233   Father God, we are told that Sunday should be a day of rest,
but we do not want to rest all day. We want to enjoy Sunday:
to enjoy meeting friends in church; being with our families;
visiting the country, seaside and parks; having friends round
for the evening; watching television; playing games. In
resting from work and school we find refreshment in leisure.

Father God, we are grateful for the opportunities of Sunday
and glad that you meet with us in them.

234   Father, we thank you for our conscious dependence on you.
You made us, you keep us, and without you our life loses its
significance. In the greatest of our achievements we know
that you are greater; in the heights of human glory, yet you
are God. We call you Father because Jesus gave us the right
so to do, because we look to you for our daily bread and
because you have given us the true bread of life that sustains
us. Therefore we thank you for our conscious dependence on
you.

And yet, in the same breath and by the same right, we thank
you for our independence. You have given us freedom; made

us individuals. You have given us the power to choose, the ability to decide. Your will is never imposed; your commandments never enforced. You draw us on to truth rather than drive us. You call us and wait, rather than demand; and when we reject you, you are long-suffering.

For our known dependence on you, praise to you, our Father. For the reality of our independence, granted in your love, praise to you, our Father.

235   Lord Jesus, our love often says:
      'I'll love you if you'll love me.'
      'I'll love you if you're sorry.'

Your love is different:
you love us as we are,
    good or bad,
    lovely or unlovely,
    right or wrong.

Help us to have such confidence in your love for us that we can dare to love others as they are.

236   Lord Jesus, we want to believe in our Father's joyful plan for the world, but such is the pressure of evil that often we are tempted to give up hope. Help us, Lord Jesus, however gloomy the forecast, never to give up hope in the possibility of fulfilment of our Father's joyful plan for us and all creation.

237   Eternal God, you are present in all our experience. Help us to learn lessons from life no matter what happens to us. In days of strength show us how to use our abilities in your service; in days of weakness and ill-health may we grow more sensitive to the problems of others; in bereavement may the

consolation you give us help us to console others. Ever give us
your strengthening power so that even life's difficulties
become occasions for praise and thanksgiving.

238   After each phrase the response is: *Come to our aid, Lord
Jesus.*

Let us pray for strength in times of temptation.

When we slip into the wrong rather than stand up for the
right, then
   Come to our aid, Lord Jesus.
When it is easier to tell a lie than speak the truth, then
   Come to our aid, Lord Jesus.
When we lose our direction in life, then
   Come to our aid, Lord Jesus.
When we neglect our prayers and worship and friends, then
   Come to our aid, Lord Jesus.
In laziness of body, mind or spirit, then
   Come to our aid, Lord Jesus.
In pain and hardship and sorrow, then
   Come to our aid, Lord Jesus.
In health and prosperity and ease, then
   Come to our aid, Lord Jesus.
In fear and loneliness and death, then
   Come to our aid, Lord Jesus.

Lord Jesus Christ, who conquered evil on the cross, give us
the power to overcome temptation and to share in your
victory, now and always.

239   Lord, you welcomed children.
In them was reflected your goodness, your openness, your
trustfulness.
You welcomed an old man and asked him to become like a
child, for children break down barriers that grown-ups
build. Their presence helps love to grow.

Lord, grant us the qualities of childhood that we may all
grow in your love.

240 Washing the feet of your disciples;
giving a cup of water to the thirsty;
healing the sick and comforting the sorrowing;
going out of your way and risking your life for others:
   this is what we learn from you, Lord.
You taught us to serve. You said that what is done for people
   in need is done for you.
In your works of compassion we see your preaching put into
   practice.
Help us to practise your way of outgoing love.
Here we are — at your service, Lord.

241 To the prayer: *Make us willing to learn,* the response is:
And give us strength to obey.

Our God, you have given us many different ways of
discovering how you want us to live.
   Make us willing to learn: *And give us strength to obey.*
You gave us Jesus, and we can find out what he said and did.
   Make us willing to learn: *And give us strength to obey.*
There is the Bible, and we can read about the experiences of
other people.
   Make us willing to learn: *And give us strength to obey.*
You can speak to us in our prayers.
   Make us willing to learn: *And give us strength to obey.*
The church, its services and meetings, can tell us about you.
   Make us willing to learn: *And give us strength to obey.*
You can teach us through people we meet and know.
   Make us willing to learn: *And give us strength to obey.*
We can be directed by the things that happen to us.
   Make us willing to learn: *And give us strength to obey.*

O God, give us the perseverance to go on discovering how
you want us to live.

242   After each phrase the response is: *Guide us and strengthen us, O Lord.*

Lord Jesus, long ago you called ordinary people like us to be your disciples, and we believe you are calling us to follow you today.

As we seek to be your faithful disciples:
   Guide us and strengthen us, O Lord.
As we face up to life's problems:
   Guide us and strengthen us, O Lord.
When we are faced with important decisions:
   Guide us and strengthen us, O Lord.
As we seek to do those things of which you would approve:
   Guide us and strengthen us, O Lord.
In choosing between what is good and what is best:
   Guide us and strengthen us, O Lord.
In our choice of friends and activities:
   Guide us and strengthen us, O Lord.
In the choice of our life's work:
   Guide us and strengthen us, O Lord.
And, above all, as we choose you to be our way, our truth and our life:
   Guide us and strengthen us, O Lord.

243   Father, in this fast and noisy world where quietness is at a premium:
   give us the patience to listen,
   the faith to hear,
   and the strength to obey.

244   Following the prayer: *Speak, O God,* the response is: *And help us to listen.*

This is a busy world, Lord:
   Speak, O God: *And help us to listen.*

Through the suffering of the sick and sad, the hungry and
the homeless, the anxious and the afraid:
    Speak, O God: *And help us to listen.*
Through the words and examples of other people:
    Speak, O God: *And help us to listen.*
Through the beauties of nature, music and art:
    Speak, O God: *And help us to listen.*
Through the Bible and the Church:
    Speak, O God: *And help us to listen.*
In the events and experiences of everyday life:
    Speak, O God: *And help us to listen.*
And when we have heard, give us strength to obey.

245   If we have been hurt by something said to us;
if we feel we have been treated unfairly;
if someone else has been chosen when we had hoped to be;
    help us not to nurse a grievance about it.

If we have tried to be helpful and no one has thanked us;
if we have put ourselves out and no one has noticed;
if we did our best but were told we had failed;
    help us not to nurse a grievance about it.

If we told the truth and were not believed;
if we have been let down by someone we trusted;
if we have supported a good cause but failed to win support;
    help us not to nurse a grievance about it.

It is so easy, Lord, to be bitter about these things, and to stop
trying. Give us a spirit like yours, so that we refuse to be put
off or discouraged.

246   We are very disobedient, Lord. We only need to know the
rules to try to get round them. In your wisdom you have not
given us a rule book, but a desire to please you.

You have shown us a life that challenges us. And you have given us a book full of stories about ordinary people and how they tried to obey.

Lord, give us imagination to see more in obedience than just doing what we are told. Help us to see it as trying our best to please you, because of your goodness and glory.

247 *For courage*

We ask, God our Father, that you will give us courage:
    courage to face disappointment without bitterness;
    courage to shoulder responsibility with cheerfulness;
    courage to hold fast to the good in the face of evil;
    courage to make experiments without being afraid of
        making mistakes;
    courage to get up when we fall, and to go forward again;
    courage to bear a good witness to Jesus Christ.
And to his name be honour and praise.

For compassion

248 Lord, you know how easy it is for us to put ourselves first. Yet we know that all around us there are people in need. The needs of some people are great and obvious, and we remember the people who have nowhere to live and the starving people who have no food. But there are other people whose needs we often overlook: the boy who has no friends, the girl who is shy, the mother who is worried about her children, the man who has problems at work.

Lord Jesus, you care for all people. Help us to be more caring and more loving. Do not let us be hard-hearted or indifferent about anyone's troubles, however large or small they may seem to be.

249   Lord, we have only so much money;
  it doesn't go far.
We have only so much time;
  we can't do everything.
We have to choose.

When we choose your way of generous love
  we call it self-denial.
How wrong we are!
Your way is the key to life and self-fulfilment.

CHRISTIAN DISCIPLESHIP

250   Lord Jesus Christ, you called to Peter, the fisherman, 'Come along with me', and Peter and his brother gave up what they were doing and followed you.

Lord, help us to hear your call to us. Make us ready to change the direction of our lives so that we follow you instead of our own selfish interests.

But, Lord, even Peter made mistakes. He did not always speak or act wisely; once he ran away and left you; once he would not admit to being your friend.

We make mistakes, too. We do not always do what you want us to do. Speak to us words of forgiveness for all our disloyalty and forgetfulness.

We remember, too, Lord, that when you left this earthly life, Peter carried on what you had been doing and worked to establish your Church on earth.

So help us to be ready to give ourselves wholeheartedly to your work, doing all that we can in your Church, so that your will is done on earth.

251 To the phrase: *Lord, in our doubts,* the response is: *Help us to find new faith.*

Father, there are many things in life that make us doubt your love.

When we see people being unkind to each other, selfish and greedy, then, Lord, in our doubts:
Help us to find new faith.

When we fail and lose confidence in ourselves, then, Lord, in our doubts:
Help us to find new faith.

When little children die and old people suffer and are in pain, then, Lord, in our doubts:
Help us to find new faith.

When people we love are unhappy and find life hard, then, Lord, in our doubts:
Help us to find new faith.

When we hear of people starving because of drought and famine, then, Lord, in our doubts:
Help us to find new faith.

When earthquakes and hurricanes make people homeless and afraid, then, Lord, in our doubts:
Help us to find new faith.

Father, in all the problems of daily living give us the faith to live courageously, in the power of your holy Spirit.

252 We all have our fears, Lord: little fears we try to overcome; big fears which threaten to dominate our lives. We are afraid of the unknown, or of illness, or of loneliness, or of what others might do to us, or of temptation, or of war. But we remember in this moment how the disciples were afraid of the storm on Lake Galilee and how you took control of their fear.

We do not ask, Lord, that you will make everything easy for

us. We must grow up; we are not spoilt children. But we do ask your help to overcome our fears.

Assure us that nothing can take your love away from us and that you will give us strength to cope and win through.

253   Father, we live our lives in little parts. There are times when the message that Jesus brought us strikes home and we live as you ask; times when the glory of life lifts us above our usual uncertainty; when the joy of living makes us want to embrace life in its fullness; or when the sight of another's needs brings out true compassion and lifts us above customary selfishness to heights from which we recognise Jesus as brother.

But there are times when the good life is like a duty hung round our necks; when we hate ourselves for turning our backs on those who plead for help, when we tread underfoot the vital spark of life and close our eyes to the vision that Jesus sets before us. It is then that we live our lives in little parts, disjointed, clumsy and lame.

Lord, grant us wholeness.
Father, lead us to maturity.
Holy Spirit of God, let us see Jesus, broken to give us
    wholeness, divided to give us unity.

254   Before God we acknowledge the problems we face when we encounter suffering in the world. Its meaning and purpose are far from clear to us. It may be that human freedom and personal responsibility are only possible when suffering is allowed to happen. It may be that perfect love can only be born through self-sacrifice and the willingness to suffer. Certainly, we see many clues in the suffering of Jesus on the cross.

Silence

May we have grace, Lord, so to follow your example and to grow in your spirit that we may bring unnecessary pain to no one; that we may strive to relieve the harsh suffering of humanity and be ready even to suffer and sacrifice ourselves for the sake of love.

255   Eternal God, it is our knowledge of your love for us that prompts our love for you; it is because you have served us in Jesus Christ that we offer service in his name; it is because you are our friend that friendship with each other means so much to us.

We offer the life of this church; its strength with its weakness. We offer ourselves; our faith with our doubt. What we offer, will you, in your mercy, take and use for the good of your kingdom.

256   Lord, we are yours, but we rarely live up to you.
Lord, we want to be yours, even when we don't live up to you.
Lord, we shall be yours — when you live in us.
Come, Lord Jesus.

257   Father, you know all about us. You share our joy in health and you understand our weakness in illness. You know how the failures of the body can tax the spirit, and how physical ailments can attack faith. You know us through and through, and in Jesus you have shared human joy and sorrow, human companionship and loneliness. You know our thoughts before we think them, and understand what we are trying to say better than we do. As you know us so well, be a comfort and guide, a strength and challenge, so that we may serve you in wholeness of body and spirit.

258   Eternal God, we act as though you were hidden from us,
your voice silent and your presence denied us. But deep
within, in the place where truth is formed and life renewed,
we know better than that. Our daily experience is your voice;
our ordinary life is the symbol of your presence; and the
universe of things, events and people proclaims your name.
Therefore we confidently dedicate all we are and know to
you.

Let life's happiness tell us of your providence.
Let human friendship whisper of your abiding love.
Let the growth of children and the ambitions of young people
    speak of human destiny.
Let the quiet pressure within which inspires us to goodness
    write hope on our hearts and lives.
Let even life's tragedies expose your will and purpose since
    the suffering of others inspires our care, the loss of others
    encourages us to give, and the sadness of others evokes our
    compassion.

Eternal God, you are never hidden from us. Your voice is
never silent, and you are always present. Therefore we
confidently dedicate all we are and know to you.

259   There are so many voices calling to us in our world today,
Lord, but one voice has spoken loud and clear.
    We offer ourselves to you now, as your faithful servants.
    We offer our minds — to think for you.
    We offer our eyes — to see the needs of others.
    We offer our voices — to speak for you.
    We offer our hands — to work for your kingdom.
    We offer our feet — to walk in your path.
    We offer our hearts — to love you above all, and to love
        others as much as we love ourselves.
    We offer our lives — to be used in your service, and to the
        glory of your name.
Accept us, bless us, and use us for your glory.

PEOPLE AROUND US

260 To the versicle: *We are grateful,* the response is: *Thank you for them, Lord.*

Thank you, Lord, for good neighbours.
For the people next door,
for our special friends,
for those we work with,
and go out with,
and who come to visit us:
    We are grateful: *Thank you for them, Lord.*

For shopkeepers and plumbers and electricians,
for policemen, bus drivers and firemen,
for road menders and rubbish collectors,
and all who work in our town/village:
    We are grateful: *Thank you for them, Lord.*

For doctors and dentists, nurses and ambulance men,
for teachers and others who help in schools,
and for the people we know at our church:
    We are grateful: *Thank you for them, Lord.*

261 *Parents and family*

Father of all families, thank you for fathers and mothers,
and for the love that our parents have given us.

Thank you for the different steps of family life:
    being cared for as a child;
    growing up and discovering ourselves;
    breaking free and living our own lives;
    finding the miracle of someone else's love;
    bringing new life into the world;
    caring for children and watching them grow.

Father of all families, thank you for our family.

262   *Friendships*

To the versicle: *Father, we thank you,* the response is:
Accept our praise.

Let us thank God for our friends.
For the way they accept us as we are, playing and relaxing
with us, Father, we thank you:
   Accept our praise.

For what our friends teach us and the way in which they
support us, Father, we thank you:
   Accept our praise.

For the joy friends give us and the pleasures they share with
us, Father, we thank you:
   Accept our praise.

For the help of good friends when we are ill or in trouble,
Father, we thank you:
   Accept our praise.

For those friends we can rely on and who are always
consistent, Father, we thank you:
   Accept our praise.

For our greatest friend, Jesus Christ, who is our Saviour and
our Lord, Father, we thank you:
   Accept our praise.

263   *Home and family*

We pray, Lord, that our home may be to us a haven of rest
and peace, a place to call our own, a community where we
belong, security for the future.

We pray, Lord, for the people in the world who are homeless,
because of war or disaster or racial prejudice.

Make us so grateful for all we have that we may use every
endeavour to ensure that each person has a home,
somewhere to call his own, and security for his future.

264 *Unhappy homes*

A short time of silence should follow each bidding.

Let us pray for homes that are unhappy:
    because of poverty, ignorance or incompetence;
    because of anxiety, sickness or sorrow;
    because of disappointment, bitterness or loneliness;
    because of quarrels between husband and wife;
    because of quarrels between parents and children;
    because of the attitudes of relatives or neighbours;
    because of the lack of any deep purpose in life;
    because of faith lost, or never found.

Lord, give us grace to help where we can, that your peace and love may abound more and more in the homes of all people.

Medical workers

265 Father, we know from the life and work of Jesus that your will is that we shall be healthy and whole. So, in confidence, we make our prayers for those whose work is for the health and healing of the community.

We pray for our own doctor, whose visits when we are ill bring comfort and reassurance. We thank you for his knowledge used for our benefit, for his unselfishness, for his dedication. Give us thankful hearts. Help us to be considerate patients so that we do not thoughtlessly add to his burden.

We pray for those whose work is in hospitals of the world: for doctors in training, for consultants and surgeons and technical staff, that in their increasing knowledge and skill they may retain humility, since all healing comes from you.

We pray for those who work behind the scenes: scientists struggling to conquer disease, workers in laboratories, those preparing and packing essential drugs.

We remember those countries where these services which we take for granted are in short supply. Lord, prompt us to be generous in responding to their need.

We pray for young people planning their career, that those so endowed with wisdom and skill may be called to use their gifts in these ways of service.

266 We remember how Jesus, through his ministry, had compassion on people who were ill, and turned that compassion into action.

We remember those who, today, continue his healing ministry. Give to doctors, we pray, patience and under-standing, and wisdom to diagnose and to prescribe. Grant to surgeons the skill, patience and poise needed in their delicate and vital tasks. Give to nurses that knowledge and gentleness which inspires confidence and helps to restore health. We pray for all medical workers, physiotherapists, secretarial staff, almoners and porters, and all who share in the battle against disease and ill-health. May each one know that he shares in the healing work of Christ.

267 *The elderly*

Father God, in whose family we are each a valued part, we pray now for those who are old. Our thoughts are especially with those who have become frail and weak; those whose eye-sight is failing; those who find it difficult to hear. We think of the lonely, with many memories but few friends to fill the long hours of the day; those who must have things done for them, when they wish so much that they could still do them for themselves; those who are house-bound, or living in hospitals or homes.

We pray for those who care for them and we pray that we ourselves may never neglect any opportunity to offer friendship and help. Teach us to be watchful for their needs and patient with their frailty and slowness, loving and serving them as honoured members of your family.

268 *Immigrants*

We call them 'foreigners' and 'immigrants', Lord —
impersonal and faceless terms. Yet, since we have one
Father, we are brothers and sisters in a common world
family. O Lord, whose compassion reached out to those of
other races, help us to welcome those who come to visit or to
live in our country, and to guide them in their difficulties. In
adjusting to our ways may they yet keep alive all that is good
in their home-life and their culture, so that, in mutual
sharing, we may learn the spirit of co-operation which makes
for peace and goodwill and the enrichment of us all.

269 *Workers*

Let us remember with sympathy those whose daily work is
monotonous: factory workers whose task is dull and
repetitive; employees whose duty makes no demands upon
them; all whose work lacks interest and satisfaction. May
God grant them patience and endurance.

Let us remember with gratitude those whose daily duty
makes life better for others: those who sweep the roads; those
who empty the dustbins; those who keep our homes clean
and tidy; those who deliver our milk and letters. May God
make us grateful and appreciative of their work.

Let us remember with concern those whose daily labour is a
burden to them: housewives who hate housework and long to
be free; children who hate school and long to leave; men who
hate their work and long for a change. May God grant them
courage and lead them into ways of greater fulfilment,
through Jesus Christ our Lord.

270 *The unemployed*

We pray for those who are unable to work because they
cannot find a job, asking that they may not lose their self-
respect, nor their pride, nor their hope. Help them to find

useful outlets for their energies and skills. Guide those in
positions of responsibility in government, commerce and
trade unions, that they may be able to channel the abilities of
those who are unemployed into useful and satisfying tasks,
so that no one may ever feel rejected or useless.

271   *Scientists*

The heavens tell out the glory of God, the vault of heaven
reveals his handiwork.

The psalmist was filled with wonder at God's work in
creation, and there are times when that is true of us. At other
times we just want to ask questions. We want knowledge, for
knowledge gives us power to control our future, to find new
ways of healing, new sources of energy, new food supplies
and new resources for leisure. Yet the very volume of
knowledge sometimes frightens us for the possibilities for
good or evil are so great.

Lord, direct with your wisdom those who are working to
extend the borders of knowledge, to solve intriguing
problems and to set us free from the limitations of ignorance.
Give us the will to influence society to use knowledge wisely
for the well-being of your people and to establish ways of
peace and justice. We look to the day when all men will
submit their knowledge to your will and, recognising your
lordship over the whole creation, will join with the psalmist
in thankful praise.

272   *The deaf*

Heavenly Father, sometimes this world seems too noisy and
we wish for silence, but we cannot imagine what a world of
silence is like. It is so difficult to think of being locked in
such a world, missing the voices of people, the beauty of
music, the happiness of laughter, the joy of friendly chatter.

Be with those who are deaf, Lord, and who miss so much.
Grant that they may be more sensitive to sight and touch, to
notice things we miss in the noise. Be with those who seek to
help: men and women who teach and nurse, doctors who
operate, family and friends who love. May we all have
understanding and love for those who are deaf.

273   *The mentally handicapped*

Father, we pray for those we call mentally handicapped,
because they do not think as we do. We do not know the deep
thoughts they have. We do know that you understand and
love them, and will give them your gift of peace. Give us, we
pray, compassion and awareness that we may be able to love
and serve any of these your children whom we meet. Bless
and guide those who work in mental hospitals and special
schools, caring for those unable to care for themselves.

274   *The disabled*

Father, give courage to the disabled and patience to those
who look after them. We admit that we often forget them.
Give us sympathy and understanding that we may care for
them in practical ways. Deepen the concern of the whole
community for the needs of disabled people, that we may
continue our Lord's work of love.

275   *The blind*

O God, we find it hard to imagine what life would be like if
we could not see. Yet many are without sight, and never
enjoy the colours of the changing seasons, the majesty of a
sunset, or the faces of those they love. We ask a special
blessing for them. If their sight cannot be restored, give them

grace to walk in darkness with you to guide them; and
prosper all research which is aimed at restoring sight, for the
sake of him who healed the sick and made the blind see.

The lonely

276 So many things in life can make us feel lonely:
　　　losing a loved one or the breaking of a friendship,
　　　being compelled by illness or infirmity to stay at home,
　　　feeling that nobody understands us,
　　　or that those around us are criticising or laughing at us.

Lord, we pray for those who are lonely today,
　　　who feel the loss of love or friendship,
　　　who feel isolated or unwanted,
　　　who fear being out of place or pushed on one side.

Give to them the rich experience of belonging to your
kingdom, and feeling at home in your family, the church.
Give to us eyes to recognise lonely people around us, and the
grace to offer friendship and love in the name of Jesus Christ,
the friend of all.

277 Lord Jesus Christ, the story of your life reminds us that you
lived closer to the poor than to the rich, nearer to the
deprived than to the privileged, and that you understood
suffering. Therefore we boldly bring to you our prayers for
the hungry and the lonely. Our own joy is touched by their
sorrow, our happiness is pierced by their sadness.

Lord Jesus, hear the cry of the hungry:
　　　the child who asks in vain for bread,
　　　the mother whose body can no longer offer nourishment to
　　　　her baby,
　　　the father, who with strong hands and willing heart has no
　　　　work to do, helpless to provide for his family.

Lord Jesus, hear the cry of the lonely:
    the widow left alone after deep companionship,
    the young person who finds it difficult to make friends,
    the family divided by homelessness,
    children lost in a broken marriage,
    those left after a severed marriage partnership.

Lord Jesus Christ, by the mystery of your coming to be one of us, enter into the sadness of the children of God to sustain them and bring them hope.

The bereaved

278   Lord, when a friend dies, part of us dies as well. But part of the friend lives on in us. Give us strength and understanding to honour and cherish that gift. Help all those who are bereaved to find the same consolation that, in the knowledge of your love, they may honour the past by looking to the future.

279   Our heavenly Father, we pray for those whose hearts have been saddened by the death of someone close and dear to them. Give to them, Father, the strong comfort which no one else can give, and let them know the comforting power of the resurrection of Jesus.

280   *Disadvantaged children*

Father, with love and anxiety we bring before you the needs of children who are the casualties of our present society:
    those made nervous, afraid or aggressive by a dominating
        and harsh experience of life;
    those caught up in the arguments and strains of tension
        between adults;

those whose home puts them at a disadvantage either by
   neglect or over-indulgence;
those so protected at home that they are ill-prepared for
   the demands of the wider world;
those unable to cope with the brutality of their
   surroundings, the ugliness of their environment, or the
   demands of an acquisitive society.

Father, you have shared with us your creative work and
entrusted us with the care of the young. Help us to grow in
sensitivity and loving kindness, insight and vision, so that
those children in our midst who are without the opportunities which are their birthright may find the encouragement and care which is their due.

281   *The exploited*

Loving God, we pray today for people who are exploited by
others:
   for people who have to work for less than a just wage;
   for people who live in fear of violence or torture;
   for people who are forced to lower their moral standards in
      order to keep their job, their home or their way of life;
   for people whose freedom of thought is denied.

Lord God, we remember that Jesus said that those who suffer
for the gospel's sake will find a place in your kingdom. Help
us to share in your work by caring for all who suffer injustice
and, wherever it is in our power, enable us to create a more
just world.

282   *The persecuted*

To the versicle: *Lord, in your mercy,* the response is: *Hear
our prayer.*

Let us pray for those in our society who are victims of others'
indifference, inhumanity or hatred.

For all deprived of their homes or livelihood by war:
  Lord, in your mercy: *Hear our prayer.*

For all who suffer slights and indignities by reason of the
colour of their skin:
  Lord, in your mercy: *Hear our prayer.*

For those imprisoned on the grounds of conscience:
  Lord, in your mercy: *Hear our prayer.*

For everyone who finds the world a hostile place in which to
live:
  Lord, in your mercy: *Hear our prayer.*

283 *Those who are cold*

We pray for those who are without warmth:
    for those who are cold in their homes, without enough
      clothes, or fuel, or warm food;
    for those who are outside in the cold because they have no
      homes;
    for those whose lives seem cold because they have no
      friends and do not know how to make friends.

Lord Jesus, you are life and love and joy; your coming brings
warmth and gaiety, purpose and peace. Come then to all who
need you, that they may know the warmth of your friendship,
and live securely in the light of your love.

Those who are ill

284 God our Father, when we are ill it is easy for us to become
frightened.
Sometimes illness is frightening because we do not know
what is wrong with us, and we feel it must be serious.
Sometimes pain is frightening because we are not used to it,
and cannot stop it.
Sometimes weakness is frightening because we feel we shall
never be strong again.

We pray for people who are frightened because they are ill.
Reassure them that, because of the knowledge which you
give to men, many diseases can now be cured. Help them to
have confidence in those with medical knowledge to diagnose
illness and to care for the sick.
When we are ill, take from us fear which will not let us
remember your loving care; and when we are well, help us
never to forget to give thanks for our health and strength.

285 Hear our prayer, Lord, for people who are ill, in hospitals, at
home, or wherever they may be. Give them courage, hope
and peace, and the knowledge that you are present in their
weakness, pain and suffering. May the skills and knowledge
of those who care for the sick be fully used to help and to
heal.

We pray especially for those who have no one to help them,
that in their loneliness they may know that you are with
them.

286 *Those who serve us*

O Lord, you have placed us in a world where we depend very
much on each other.
We thank you for the many people who work to make our
lives more comfortable and enjoyable.
We remember with gratitude those who come to our homes:
the postman, the milkman, the dustman.
We think of those who work to provide us with electricity,
gas, oil and coal; those who serve in shops, drive buses and
trains, control our roads, and those involved in communica-
tions.
There are so many and we acknowledge that our lives are
enriched by their work. May they find purpose and
satisfaction in knowing that their work contributes to the
well-being of all.

Those in industry and commerce

287 We remember those who invent, manufacture and sell the world's goods, and on whom our lives depend.

Let us pray for all workers torn by conflict in their employment:
  who are caused hardship by strikes and disputes;
  who are prevented from doing an honest day's work for an
    honest day's pay:
in silence let us hold them in the love of God.

Let us pray for those whose grievances are genuine:
  who labour in poor conditions;
  who are denied their rights;
  who are carelessly employed;
  who are over-worked and under-paid:
in silence let us hold them in the care of God.

Let us pray for those who shirk their work:
  who seek selfishly to gain without effort;
  who cause unnecessary trouble and prevent good progress;
  who have a grudge both against work and against
    management:
in silence let us hold them in the good influence of God.

Let us pray for trade unions,
  and for all boards and councils for industrial relations;
  for industrial chaplains concerned that Christian
    principles should motivate all policies and decisions:
in silence let us hold them in the guidance of God.

Let us pray for those whose job is to sell what industry produces:
  for salesmen, shopkeepers and assistants;
  for owners of small businesses;
  for those in large undertakings:
in silence let us hold them in the purpose of God.

Father God, you invite us to be your fellow-workers; deliver us from misunderstanding and readiness to condemn when we are inconvenienced. Free us from all greed and waste, and help us to care for others as you care for all.

288   A period of silence is kept after each bidding.

Let us pray for management and employees, praying for:
  peace in industrial life;
  justice, which is the forerunner of peace;
  insight to understand what is vital in any matter needing
    decision;
  reasonableness to see the other man's point of view;
  forgiveness of wrongs done;
  grace to give as much as we expect to receive;
  humility to remember that Christ is our Master, and that
    we are all brothers and sisters in him.

289   *Trade unions*

To the versicle: *Lord, in your mercy,* the response is: *Hear
our prayer.*

Let us pray for the Trade Union Movement of this country,
that it may work for the true well-being of all working
people, use its power with wisdom, and make its demands
based on justice for all people.
  Lord, in your mercy: *Hear our prayer.*

Let us pray for the Trade Union Congress and its officers,
that it may wisely use its influence upon the government and
upon each trade union to work towards industrial peace and
goodwill.
  Lord, in your mercy: *Hear our prayer.*

Let us pray for the officers, presidents, general secretaries
and shop stewards of every trade union that they may be
concerned in improving the lot of their members and
pursuing the welfare and peace of all people.
  Lord, in your mercy: *Hear our prayer.*

Let us pray for all working people that they may always be
willing to do good work and give good service, and to find in
their work a rôle of service to all people.
  Lord, in your mercy: *Hear our prayer.*

EDUCATION

290 *Pre-school children*

Dear Father God, we thank you for all the happiness of play-
group:
    with our legs we can run and jump and dance and climb;
    with our hands we can build and draw and cut and play;
    with our eyes we can see books and pictures and colours
        and other children;
    with our lips we can talk and sing and smile at our friends;
    sometimes we can be very quiet and still.

Dear Father God, we thank you that in all the happiness of
playgroup, its fun and noise and quietness, we can know that
you are near.

291 *Our schools*

Almighty God, it is your purpose that all should have the
opportunity to lead a full and rich life. As we give you our
thanks for schools, so we pray for the teachers and children
in the schools we know: for those who accept the
responsibility of guiding our children in their search for
knowledge, and for the children whose minds are beginning
to awaken to the wonders and mysteries and problems of life.
May the power of your presence be in each school
community, in all the counsel which our children are given,
in the friendships they form. Add to their growing knowledge
the wisdom that comes only from you.

292 *School and college*

Father God, we remember and pray for the children and
young people of this country in their daily learning.

We think of children who are spending their first hours away
from home in nursery school, infant school or play-group:
    those who are eager and active as they explore and
        welcome new experiences and new relationships,
    those more shyly weighing up their first steps,
    those who cannot enjoy physical exercise and those who
        cannot learn in ordinary ways.

We think of children who, advancing in knowledge and
learning, face choices which are crucial for the rest of their
lives:
    those for whom the choices seem unreal and unrelated to
        the rest of their experience,
    those growing in confidence, enjoying learning and
        gaining a wider experience of life through school,
    those defeated by an unsympathetic system and silently
        longing for real and personal relationships,
    those in the final years at school and facing important
        decisions about their future.

We think of young people whose ability and circumstances
allow them to accept the opportunity of further education:
    those meeting college or university for the first time and
        finding their values tested and their horizons widened,
    those who link industry or commerce with education as
        they follow a day release course or an apprenticeship,
    those for whom education seems an end in itself yielding
        no clear direction for the future.

Father God, we think of all children and young people,
praying that they may be worthy of the best in our society,
and society worthy of their potential.

293   *Religious education*

We remember, Father, those who are involved in religious
education in schools everywhere, and particularly the schools
of our own neighbourhood. We pray for the teachers, that in

their work of preparation and teaching, and in their relationships with their pupils, they may be blessed and encouraged by the help of your Spirit. We pray for the pupils, that in the search for truth, in the study of the ideas of great men and women, and in the words and deeds of Jesus Christ, they may find meaning and purpose for their lives.

294 *Teachers*

Heavenly Father, we pray for teachers and leaders in our schools. Give to them patience, understanding and vision that they may inspire their pupils in the pursuit of learning. We remember in our prayers those who witness to Jesus Christ in the community of the school; may the influence of their lives guide others into paths of truth, through Jesus Christ, who is the way, the truth and the life.

295 *Colleges and universities*

Lord God, you are truth: guide we pray all those who in universities and colleges are seeking truth. Give them grace to lay aside all prejudice, the will to forsake all easy ways, and the discipline not to be content with partial knowledge. Be with those who teach and those who learn that together they may discover the greatness of your works.

Learning and working

296 Lord Jesus, when you were here among men, many came to ask you the way of life, and none who came went away unanswered. We, who are bewildered by so many things in this modern world, come to you now, seeking to know what is your will for us, and praying that we, too, may hear your voice and be obedient.

297   A selection may be made from the following biddings, allowing a period of silence after each one used. The silence can be drawn to a close with the prayer: *Almighty God, use our concern,* to which the response is: *To strengthen those for whom we pray.*

Let us pray:

> for teachers, lecturers and professors who by their work shape the lives of others, direct the course of learning and enrich our living;

> for the young participating in institutions as part of their personal development and education, and also for those who are strained by, or cannot cope with, the involvement of the young;

> for schools in this and other countries where there are not enough teachers, and for children deprived of a stable relationship with a teacher and the broadening and developing influence of education;

> for churches trying to be learning and teaching communities of children and adults, that their educational programme will help to set people free to grow to their fullness as persons and as the children of God;

> for those who accept responsibility in the church's name to lead and help in children's groups, that they may work with imagination, care and growing faith;

> for those who hear and accept God's call to work overseas, that they may feel supported by the care and prayer of those who commissioned them and be heartened by the responsiveness of those they teach;

> for the whole work of education that it may point away from privilege and self-seeking towards peace and justice and the shaping of the kingdom of love in society;

for the church, that it may take its responsibility as an educator, its ability to influence state education, and its opportunities to pave the way for dialogue between differeing church traditions with greater seriousness;

for the Minister of State and his staff, school governors and managers, and all who are involved in administration, that they may be given courage to provide the greatest opportunities to the largest number.

COMMUNITY LIFE

298 *Stable government*

Let us thank God for the benefits of stable government and the provisions of community life.
  For police who guard our freedom and maintain good order;
  for schools where children and young people prepare for life;
  for hospitals where the sick and diseased are cared for;
  for good roads enabling us to travel;
  for the efficient disposal of rubbish and unwanted waste;
  for parks and gardens full of beauty and colour;
  for libraries full of books; for magazines and papers;
  for theatres and community centres for our enjoyment;
  for evening classes and all opportunities to learn new skills;
  for the care and welfare of the deprived;
  we praise and thank you, heavenly Father.

Grant, O Lord, that we may be grateful for all the benefits we receive, watchful to ensure fairness and justice in local affairs, and conscientious in playing our part as good citizens.

299 *God's world*

Lord, this is your world; and it is ours.
There is food to share; or to make us greedy.
There is air to breathe; or to pollute.
There are homes able to welcome; or to exclude.
There are cars to carry us; or to kill.
There are people to love; or to hate.

Lord, in your world, which is also ours, you have given us the
ability to choose. Help us to make right choices.

300 *Relationships*

Following the phrase: *In all this trouble,* the response is:
Grant us your peace, Lord.

Lord, this is a world of violence and upset: race against race;
ideology against ideology; colour against colour; interest
against interest.
In all this trouble: *Grant us your peace, Lord.*

Lord, ours is a nation of unrest: industrial argument; class
distinction; political debate; racial tension; generation gaps;
criminal activity.
In all this trouble: *Grant us your peace, Lord.*

Lord, we are people at odds: not good at getting on with
others; sometimes not even with our own family; finding
relationships difficult with different generations, different
attitudes, different responses, different characters.
In all this trouble: *Grant us your peace, Lord.*

And, Lord, we are people involved in personal crisis: we lose
loved ones; we become ill; situations change; disasters befall;
tensions arise; and difficulties come.
In all this trouble: *Grant us your peace, Lord.*

Lord, we do not ask to be immune from trouble, but to have
your peace even in the midst of the troubles of the world.

301 *The government and those who rule*

To the versicle: *Lord, hear us,* the response is: *Lord, graciously hear us.*

Lord God, in whose hands are the destinies of men and of nations, we bring before you in our prayers those who have been entrusted with special responsibilities for the life of our nation.

For our Queen, that she may uphold all that is best in our common life:
Lord, hear us: *Lord, graciously hear us.*

For our Prime Minister, and other leaders of political thought, that you will grant them wisdom and integrity:
Lord, hear us: *Lord, graciously hear us.*

For our own Member of Parliament, that he/she may care deeply for the well-being of the constituency:
Lord, hear us: *Lord, graciously hear us.*

For all who undertake the tasks of local government, that they may devote special attention to those who cannot look after themselves:
Lord, hear us: *Lord, graciously hear us.*

302 *Local government*

Lord God, ruler of the world, we thank you for those who are skilled in the administration of local government and we pray for those who serve us in this community. With all the demands made upon them, and with all the specialised knowledge they need, may those in positions of authority and leadership not lose sight of the purpose of their work — that people may be helped to live together usefully and happily in this community. May all the rules and regulations be administered with understanding and care for individuals, so that all may feel that they are needed, and each may know that he matters.

CONTRIBUTORS

John Allcott
F.W. Bakewell
Roy Chapman
Levi Dawson
Leslie Earnshaw
Paul Eddyshaw
Jennifer Franklin
Brian Goss
Anthony Green
Gilbert Griffin
Paul Harrison
David Hawkes
C.W. Herbert
Donald Hilton
Harry B. Howard
Martin Howie
Edmee Hurst
Edward Jacson
Margaret Jarman
Glyn Jenkins
Brother Kenneth
Margaret Kitson

Chris Lammiman
Marjorie Lewis
Kenneth Mumford
Marian Musselwhite
Roy Newell
David Owen
Tony Perry
John Petty
Michael Quicke
John Reardon
Derek and Mavis Richmond
Hazel Snashall
Guy Stanford
John Sutcliffe
Stephen Thornton
Peter Tongeman
Kenneth Wadsworth
Donald Wilkins
Brian Wren
Jack and Edna Young

Rodborough Bede Book

INDEX

Adoration
  Boyhood of Jesus 43
  Christian life-style 228
  Christmas 16-19
  Church - community 132, 134-136
  Church - life and mission 170
  Disciples of Jesus 57
  Easter 98
  Epiphany 16, 17
  Good Friday 84
  Harvest 194-195
  Jesus the friend 61
  Lent - general 33-34
  Palm Sunday 77-78
  Passiontide 84
  Pentecost 107
  Trinity 116
  World about us 221
Advent
  Invocation 1-4
  Penitence 5-8
  Supplication 9-11
All Souls 149
Anger 231

Baptism
  of an infant 208
  of an adult 209
Bereaved 278-279
Bible 8, 206
Blind 275

Celebration 115, 120
Children 147, 154-155, 239, 280
  Baptism 208
  Dedication 210
  Promotion 211
Christ (Jesus)
  Birth 12-16, 18-19, 22, 24, 26-27
  Boyhood 43-46, 154
  Example 41, 60, 70, 85, 240, 254
  Followers 33, 57-60, 113, 149, 153
  Friendship 61-63, 235
  Healer 72-75
  Light, The 9, 14, 17
  Life and work 11, 126, 130
  Ministry 35, 38, 42, 52, 96
  Teacher 64-71
  Temptations 50-55
  Worker 47-49
Christian aid 171, 178-182
Christian life-style
  Adoration 228
  Caring 248

Childlike 239
Courage 247
Dedication 249
Dependence on God 234
Discipleship 242
Freedom 228
Fruit of the Spirit 230
General 139, 162, 229, 231, 241, 243
In time of temptation 238
Kindness 111
Love 110, 235
Obedience 246
Penitence 229-232
Service 138, 237, 240
Sunday 233
Supplication 236-248
Thanksgiving 234-235
Wonder 135
Christmas
  Invocation 2-4, 12-15
  Adoration 16-19
  Penitence 6
  Thanksgiving 20-24
  Supplication 25-28
  Intercession 29-32
Church
  Anniversary 192
  Children's workers 156
  Community 106, 119-120, 122-125, 141, 143-145, 147-148, 150-151, 153-155, 157-159, 172, 215
  in all the world 121, 145, 149, 174-177
  its ministry 129, 158, 161
  its mission 171, 173-176, 181-182
  its worship 122-124, 127, 131, 150, 168-170, 215
  unity of 187-189
College 292, 295
Commerce 287
Community 298
Compassion 248
Courage 91, 96, 247
Creation 215-216
  (see also God: Creator)

Daily life 28, 102, 125, 131, 146, 157, 217, 223, 237, 244, 251, 286
Deaf 272
Dedication
  of children 147, 210
  of gifts 161, 163-167

of ourselves   162, 186, 249, 255-259
Developing countries   183-184
Disabled   274
Disciples   57-59, 242
   (see also Christ: Followers)
Discipleship   250-259
Doctors   265-266

Easter
   Invocation   97, 130
   Adoration   98
   Thanksgiving   99-102
   Supplication   103
   New life   104
Education   290-297
Elderly   267
Epiphany
   Invocation   13-14
   Adoration   16-17
   Thanksgiving   23
   Supplication   25, 27-28

Faith   69, 91
Family life   44, 46, 157, 261
Fear   252
Festival, church   192
Forgiveness - see Penitence
Freedom   228
Friends   63, 73, 124, 143, 262
Fruit of the Spirit   230

God
   Creator   39, 135-136, 152, 194-195, 217-218, 271
   Dependence upon   234
   Fatherhood   128
   Greatness of   132, 221
   Gifts, His   139, 145
   In the world   42
   Peace of   131, 300
   Presence of   133, 142, 158, 258
Good Friday
   Adoration   83-84
   Penitence   79, 85-86
   Thanksgiving   87-89
   Supplication   90-95
   Intercession   96
Government   298, 301
Grievances   245
Grown-ups   148
Guidance   242

Harvest (see also God: Creator; and World about us)
   Adoration   194-195

Thanksgiving   196-199
Intercession   199-201, 271
Dedication   161
Healing, Ministry of   72, 74-75, 265-266, 284-285
Holidays   146, 226
Holy Communion   212-213
Holy Spirit - see Pentecost
Holy Week   76-96
Home   263-264
Homeless   263
Hope   236
Hospitals   265-266
Human creativity   217-219
Human values   102
Humble spirit   134

Ill people   284-285
Immigrants   268
Independence   234
Industry   287-288
Injustice   171
Insight   225
Intercession
   Baptism   208-209
   Bereaved   278-279
   Blind   275
   Children   280
   Christian aid   179-180
   Christmas and Epiphany   29-32
   Church Community   157-160
   Cold   283
   College   292, 295
   Deaf   272
   Dedication (of a child)   210
   Developing countries   183-184
   Disabled   274
   Education   297
   Elderly people   267
   Exploited people   281
   Friends   63
   Good Friday and Passiontide   96
   Government   301-302
   Harvest   199, 201
   Healing   74-75
   Home and family   263-264
   Illness   284-285
   Immigrants   268
   Lent   48-49, 56, 63, 74-75
   Life and mission   174-177
   Lonely people   276
   Medical workers   265-266
   Mentally handicapped   273
   Palm Sunday   82
   Peacemakers   205
   Pentecost   114

People around us 277
Persecuted people 282
Promotion 211
Refugees 181-182
Relationships 300
Religious education 293
Schools 291-292, 295
Scientists 271
Teachers 294
Trade Unions 289
Unemployed 270
Work and workers 48-49, 269, 287-289
Invocation
  Advent 1-4
  Christmas 2-4, 12-15
  Church Community 119-133
  Easter 97
  Epiphany 13-14
  Palm Sunday 76
  Pentecost 105-106
  Trinity 115

Jesus - see Christ
Justice 184

Kingdom of God 172
Kindness 111

Leisure 233
Lent (see also Christ)
  Adoration 33-34, 43, 57, 61
  Penitence 35-37, 44, 50-51, 64
  Thanksgiving 38-39, 45, 52, 58, 62, 65-67, 72
  Supplication 40-42, 46-47, 53-55, 59-60, 68-70, 73
  Intercession 48-49, 56, 63, 74-75
  Meditation 71
  Dedication 249
Local government 301-302
Loneliness 157, 276
Love 110, 235, 240

Mary, mother of Jesus 191
Medical workers 265-266
Meditation
  ministry of Jesus 96, 254
  on words of Jesus 71
Mentally handicapped 273
Mission - see Church
Mothering Sunday 190-191
Mothers 190

Need, Those in 30-32, 96, 178-182, 199, 248, 277, 282

New discoveries 214, 227
New life 104, 127, 144
New year 185-186

Obedience 241, 246
Offertory - see Dedication
Old people - see Elderly
Outings 146

Palm Sunday
  Invocation 76
  Adoration 77-78
  Penitence 81
  Thanksgiving 81
  Supplication 80-81
  Intercession 82
Parents 207, 261
Parliament 301
Passiontide
  Adoration 83-84
  Penitence 79, 85-86
  Thanksgiving 81, 87-89
  Supplication 90-95
  Intercession 96
Peacemakers 203, 205
Penitence
  Advent 5-8
  Christian aid 171
  Christian life-style 229-232
  Church Community 137-141
  Church unity 187
  Good Friday 85-86
  Lent 35-37, 44, 50-51, 64
  Palm Sunday 79, 81
  Passiontide 79, 85-86
  Remembrance day 202
Pentecost
  Invocation 105-106
  Adoration 107
  Thanksgiving 108-109
  Supplication 110-113, 173, 216
  Intercession 114
People 221, 260, 277, 281-283
Peter, apostle 250
Play-group 290
Prime Minister 301
Promotion time 211

Queen 301
Quietness 243

Refugees 181-182
Religious education 293
Remembrance Sunday 202-205
Resurrection - see Easter

Seasons   104, 222-223
Selfishness   137
Seven Last Words   94
School   156, 291-293
Skills   219
Space exploration   227
Spring   104
Sunday   119, 150, 233
Supplication
  Advent   9-11
  Baptism   207
  Care of children   155
  Children's workers   156
  Christian life-style   236-248
  Christmas and Epiphany   25-28
  Church Community   133, 151-157,
    239, 241
  Church unity   189
  Compassion   248
  Courage   247
  Daily life   157, 237, 244
  Discipleship   59-60,   65,   68-69,
    153, 242, 250-253
  Easter   103-104
  Good Friday and Passiontide   90-
    95
  Grievance   245
  Harvest   200, 224
  Human creativity   219
  Hope   236
  Learning   296
  Lent   40-42, 46-47, 53-55, 59-60,
    65, 68-70, 73
  Life and mission   172-173, 176
  Love   240
  New discoveries   216
  New year   185
  Obedience   246
  Palm Sunday   80-81
  Parents   207
  Pentecost   110-113, 216
  Pre-school children   154
  Quietness   243
  Remembrance day   204
  Service   73
  Temptation   238
  World about us   224-225, 299

Teachers   156, 291, 293-294, 297
Temptation   50-54, 56, 238
Thanksgiving
  All Souls   149
  Bible   206
  Children   147, 290
  Christ (Jesus)   45, 52, 66-67

Christian aid   178
Christian life-style   234-235
Christmas and Epiphany   20-24
Church Community   141-145, 192
Church unity   188
Daily life   286
Disciples   58
Easter   99-102
Family life   261
Friendship   62, 262
General   150
Good Friday and Passiontide   87-
  89
Government   298
Grown-ups   148
Harvest   196-199
Healing   72
Holidays   226
Human creativity   217-218
Lent   38-39, 45, 52, 58, 62, 66-67,
  72
Love   235
Mothers   190-191
New discoveries   214, 227
Outings   146, 226
Palm Sunday   81
Peacemakers   203
Pentecost   108-109, 216
People around us   260
Service   286
Touch   220
Trinity   117-118
World about us   215, 222-223, 286
Young people   193
Touch   220
Trade Unions   289
Trinity
  Invocation   115
  Adoration   116, 134
  Penitence   50
  Thanksgiving   117-118

Unemployed   270
Unhappy homes   264
Unity, Church   187-189
University   292, 295

Wonder   135
Work, Daily   47-49, 201, 269, 286
Workers   269
World about us   104, 135-136, 215,
  221-222, 224-225, 271, 299-300

Young people   193